"*Taking Sexy Back* is going directly on my top list of reco[m] only did I learn a lot, but I also enjoyed the ease, directness guides us to deeper sexual and relational self-awareness. *A*

—**Esther Perel**, couples therapist, TED speaker, host of the hit podcast *Where Should We Begin?*, and author of *Mating in Captivity* and *The State of Affairs*

"In these enlightening and powerful pages, Alexandra Solomon provides a clear path to thinking about our sexuality in the context of our psyches, our relationships, and our pleasure. There are countless books on relationships and countless books on sexuality, but never have I seen a book that asks us to examine our sexual lives in such a holistic, empowering, and eye-opening way. This is a rare and life-changing gift for women everywhere."

—**Lori Gottlieb**, *New York Times* bestselling author of *Maybe You Should Talk to Someone*

"Psychologist Alexandra Solomon (*Loving Bravely*) empowers and enlightens in this manual that encourages women to accept and control their sexuality… Like a wise older sister or a trusted friend, Solomon illustrates how to move from fear to love… She also tackles the topic of sexual traumas and the poison they inject into relationships, and encourages experimentation and sexual fantasies as tools to learn one's own sexuality… Solomon proves to be a savvy, empathetic voice in this educational and inspiring guide."

—*Publishers Weekly*

"When the next sexual revolution comes, this book will certainly be among its founding documents. It takes the best parts of what psychology has learned about love and sex, and distills them to their simplest human essence. Love and sex, as the author notes, are a powerful and ancient magic, and this book will do much to help the next generation of women claim more of this magic for themselves."

—**Stephen Snyder, MD**, host of the *Relationship Doctor* podcast on Macmillan Publishers' QDT Network, and author of *Love Worth Making*

"In Alexandra Solomon's book, *Taking Sexy Back*, she asks us to dig deep, to look beyond our assumptions, to shift from being sexualized to being sexual, and to find our erotic selves under years of cultural repression. This book helps women to reclaim their inherent right to their sexuality, which we all need as we move into the next wave of empowering ourselves, fighting for our right to feel pleasure in our own bodies—without guilt, shame, or remorse. I will pass Solomon's wise advice on to my own daughter."

—**Tammy Nelson, PhD**, certified sex and relationship therapist, and author of *Getting the Sex You Want* and *The New Monogamy*

"Have you ever wished you knew someone that combined the intimacy of your best friend with the skills and competency of a PhD in psychology? Someone who could support you on the road to creating a wildly fulfilling sex life—both with yourself and your partner(s)? This book will change your life, open doors, and allow you to own every drop of the hot, sexy woman you were born to become."

> —**Regena Thomashauer (aka Mama Gena)**, founder and CEO of The School of Womanly Arts at www.mamagenas.com, and *New York Times* bestselling author of *Pussy*

"*Taking Sexy Back* welcomes women into an adventurous reclamation of our sexuality as just that—*ours!* And *ours* alone."

> —**Linda Kay Klein**, author of *PURE*, and founder of Break Free Together

"With grace, savvy, and compassion, Solomon dismantles the web of erroneous messages that stand in the way of sexual fulfillment for countless women. *Taking Sexy Back* is a powerful, much-needed guide to reclaiming your sexuality and blossoming into your fullest, most pleasure-capable self."

> —**August McLaughlin**, media personality, podcast host/producer, and author of *Girl Boner*

"Chock-full of poignant real-life stories, scientific data presented in an accessible format, and questions to provoke deeper thinking, *Taking Sexy Back* is what *every* woman needs to set her on the path to sexual empowerment and fulfillment. It is the only book of its kind written in a wonderfully inclusive way, encompassing the experiences of those who identify as straight, lesbian, bisexual, cisgender, gender-queer, monogamous, nonmonogamous, and more. Solomon's passion and compassion for women's sexual discovery shines through. I will be recommending this book to students, clients, and friends for years to come."

> —**Laurie Mintz, PhD**, professor in the department of psychology at the University of Florida, and author of *A Tired Woman's Guide to Passionate Sex* and *Becoming Cliterate*

Taking Sexy Back

How to Own Your Sexuality & Create the Relationships You Want

ALEXANDRA H. SOLOMON, PhD

NEW HARBINGER PUBLICATIONS, INC.

Publisher's Note

Distributed in Canada by Raincoast Books

Copyright © 2020 by Alexandra H. Solomon
New Harbinger Publications, Inc.
5674 Shattuck Avenue
Oakland, CA 94609
www.newharbinger.com

"Basson's Model of Sexual Motivation," in chapter 5, from R. Basson (2002). "Rethinking Low Sexual Desire in Women." *BJOG: An International Journal of Obstetrics & Gynecology* 109: 357–363. Used by permission of John Wiley & Sons, Inc.

"River of Integration" figure, in chapter 6, from the work of Daniel Siegel. Used by permission of the author.

"Could You Just Love Me Like This" by Hollie Holden copyright © 2016 by Hollie Holden (http://www.hollieholden.me). Reprinted by permission of the author.

Cover design by Sara Christian; Acquired by Jess O'Brien; Edited by Marisa Solis

Library of Congress Cataloging-in-Publication Data on file

Printed in the United States of America

21	20	19								
10	9	8	7	6	5	4	3	2	1	First Printing

Our erotic knowledge empowers us, becomes a lens through which we scrutinize all aspects of our existence, forcing us to evaluate those aspects honestly in terms of their relative meaning in our lives.

—Audre Lorde, *Sister Outsider: Essays and Speeches*

This book is dedicated to my students and clients, past, present, and future, who are some of my most inspiring teachers. Thank you for sharing you with me. I am better for knowing you.

Contents

PART III: **Your Sexy Is Here to Stay**

Foreword

Over the last two decades, research in the area of human sexuality has made one thing very clear. *Regardless of women's country of origin, age, socioeconomic status, sexual orientation, relationship status, and education, a lot of women experience chronic sexual problems.* In fact, about one in three women will have lasting sexual difficulties that cannot be attributed to a short-term stressor, illness, or medication side effects.

When one-third of women are sexually dissatisfied—a problem that is more common than the prevalence of chronic pain, diabetes, or depression—we need to figure out what's going on! Many women lack accurate information about sexuality. This might be due to a failure of the education system to teach sex education, or perhaps it is due to restrictive attitudes about sex in women's early environments. Too many women hold false, inaccurate, misleading, distressing, damaging, and life-altering beliefs about sex. Many women feel that they cannot talk to a primary care doctor about sex, and there is no road map for how to navigate the unregulated online information.

When *Taking Sexy Back* arrived in my inbox, I found myself nodding by the second paragraph. By the fourth I had made a list of the different venues in which I would use the book, including with clients, in teaching students, in training health care providers, and as a reference in my own research and writing. And by the end of chapter 1, I had highlighted in yellow nearly every line.

"It's time for women to construct their sexuality from the inside-out," Alexandra Solomon celebrates. This means getting to know, fully and in the most intimate way, your feelings, wants, and desires when it comes to your own sexuality. Rather than leaving it there as a lofty far-away delusion, Solomon walks us through exactly how to get there. By tackling sexual harassment and violence head-on and unapologetically, we take on the position that if we cannot say no, then we cannot truly ever say yes. And to that, Solomon provides examples of what consent does, and what it most definitely does not, look like.

I love love love that relational self-awareness is emphasized early on, with encouragement to move toward an experience of ourselves that is more authentic by paying attention, leaving judgment at the door, and being true to ourselves and what we believe. We are asked to probe deep and ask emotional questions, such as "How does my relationship with my body enhance or constrain my sexual experiences?" and "To what degree is sex a source of pleasure and play?" I believe firmly that if we were to ask ourselves such questions at the earliest stages of discovering our own sexuality, years, if not decades, of pain and judgment about feeling inadequate with sex would be spared. I would like to gift *Taking Sexy Back* to every young woman I know, including my own daughter.

Though *Taking Sexy Back* is written for women, it weaves diversity throughout its pages beautifully. Solomon dismantles gender reveal parties unapologetically (thank goodness!). In that way, it is for everyone, not just women whose birth sex matches their current gender identity. In fact, we know that individuals who have trans or nonbinary experiences are even more likely than cisgender individuals to face hostility about sex, and to especially lack adequate sex education. *Taking Sexy Back* is for all bodies and flavors of being a woman.

Because so many women feel alone in their sexual concerns, it can be immensely validating to meet other women having similar issues. This is part of what makes group sex therapy so magical! In *Taking Sexy Back*, Solomon shares stories of real women and real sexual concerns in every chapter. As you read these stories, pay attention to your reactions and whether there are any that resonate with you. I believe that for women who are uncomfortable or unable to share their issues with a health care provider, pointing them to a page in the book that describes a person with similar sexual issues can be incredibly validating for the woman and useful for the care provider. And just as the chapters are chock-full of personal stories and solutions, the pages are also filled with data and findings from scientific studies. The reader should rest assured that the statistics provided were backed by rigorous scientific approaches.

Solomon presents questions with Our Sexy in mind in every chapter. I wish for every woman to be handed a list of these questions when they come of age, and that they honor their inner sexual goddesses in responding to each and every one of them. If we could achieve that goal, I truly believe the current staggering figures of 1 in 3 women with sexual problems would reduce to 1 in 100 women. This book is a gift for women and for the people who love them.

—Lori A. Brotto, PhD, author of
Better Sex Through Mindfulness

PART I

Preparing for the Journey

From Outside-In
to Inside-Out

Today our sexuality is an open-ended personal project;
it is part of who we are, an identity, and no longer merely something we do.

—Esther Perel, *Mating in Captivity*

I am so freaking glad you're here! This book is the culmination of thousands of hours of conversations and innumerable long days and late nights spent with my laptop. I wrote this book with the unflagging support of a kick-ass team of editors, consultants, and graduate and undergraduate students, and you need to know right off the bat how much we have been thinking about *you*. We have been worrying about you. We have been feeling protective of you. We have been laughing and crying and imagining how you'd respond to these pages. And now you're here.

You are about to do something that is both challenging and exhilarating. You are going to deepen your understanding of who you are sexually. *This process, however, is less discovery and more reclamation— taking back that which is your birthright as a woman and as a person.* This book will help you rewrite the troubling and shame-loaded stories our culture has placed on that tender and essential part of you: your sexuality. The journey of this book is *both* personal *and* universal. Women walk the path both alone and together. The path that leads *away* from silence, shame, and isolation *toward* pleasure, empowerment, and connection.

This book is written for every woman who has:

- remained silent because she didn't know how to open up to her intimate partner about her sexual preferences, needs, and desires

- struggled to stay present and engaged during a sexual experience

- had sexual experiences that left her feeling sad or disconnected from her authentic self

- beaten herself up for sexual choices she has made or not made

- felt anxious about the fluidity of her sexuality

- been let down by a system of sex education that left gaps in her understanding and shame for knowing she needed more information

- faked an orgasm because she didn't know what else to do

- felt disconnected from, or ashamed about, the most intimate parts of her body.

This is a book about self-awareness. Self-awareness that guides you toward sexual choices that are enlivening and uplifting. Self-awareness that helps you celebrate your sexuality as essential, imperfect, and *yours*.

I have been working as a professor and a relationship therapist for over twenty years, and what I know for sure is that we are long overdue for some vulnerable and perhaps difficult conversations about our sexual selves. Our culture treats sex as either titillating or taboo, which makes it so hard to talk about sex in a curious and wholehearted way and which leaves most of us with sexual shame that compromises our individual and relational well-being.

The relationship you have with yourself is the foundation of all of your relationships. *Although sex is something you (usually) experience with another person, your sexuality is yours.* Your sexuality is much more than to whom you are attracted or what you do or don't do in bed. It is a central part of who you are, and it is about how you navigate the physical, emotional, spiritual, and intellectual need for pleasure, closeness, and connection. This book is a journey toward greater *sexual self-awareness* centered on the relationship between you and your sexuality.

The Old Way: Outside-In Sexuality

There is a world of difference between being *sexualized* and being *sexual*.[1] Sexualization is a position of passivity, and it is the sad reality for girls and women in this culture. Women and feminine-presenting people are flooded with stories from family, friends, religious institutions, school, the media, and pornography about who and how they ought to be sexually. These voices are loud and opinionated, and they crowd out a woman's ability to hear her own voice. Sexualization obliterates women's agency, reducing them—their experiences, thoughts, feelings, and power—to one-dimensional sexual objects who perform their sexuality the "right" way or the "wrong" way.

When our culture positions men as active/subject/predator and women as passive/object/prey, women's sole access point to their own sexuality is as a reflection in the eyes of another. *This toxic climate robs women of sexual autonomy and self-definition, leaving them with only an outside-in experience of their sexuality.* This toxic climate yields a dating culture in which sexual experiences all too often involve poor or absent communication and insufficient empathy and care. And this toxic climate sets the stage for couples to struggle with sexual desire.

Women are taught to be sexually appealing but not demanding, to be sexually available but not hungry, to bring our partners to orgasm but to fake our own pleasure for their benefit and protection. Many of us cannot name our sexual anatomy or describe what those parts long for. The sad truth is that although women are more empowered than ever, that agency doesn't necessarily follow us into the bedroom. *Women's sexual experiences are not as good/positive/rewarding/pleasurable as they could be and should be.* Perhaps a part of us knows that moving from silence into voice will shake the very foundation of patriarchy. And what happens then?

The New Way: Inside-Out Sexuality

It's time to flip the script and shift from sexualized to sexual. It's time for women to construct their sexuality from the inside-out. Instead of awaiting or fearing the label, "you're sexy," it's time to get to know "Your Sexy." Your Sexy is your sexuality—the unfolding story of your relationship to the erotic. Your Sexy is connected in an ancestral way to every woman/witch/goddess/bitch/heroine who came before.

It is time to quiet the noise of the outside world so you can create, from the inside-out, a deeper connection to Your Sexy and reclaim that which has always been yours. Neither earned nor ordained by another, an inside-out experience of Your Sexy is about believing that your sexuality connects to and reflects your physical, emotional, intellectual, and spiritual self. By cultivating an inside-out experience of Your Sexy, you courageously step outside narrow gender roles and insist on nothing less than self-aware and empowered sexual experiences. Shifting from an outside-in to an inside-out experience of Your Sexy is the shift:

- from performance to enjoyment

- from shame to comfort

- from numb to enlivened

- from restrictive to expansive.

A sexual experience might express "I love you," it might express "I need comfort," it might express "I want to make a baby," it might express "I want to try something I've never tried before," and a thousand more things. Experiencing Your Sexy from the inside-out infuses those expressions with integrity, making every yes a heartfelt yes.

I work with so many long-term couples for whom sex is a tremendously fraught topic. While a commitment to sexual self-awareness does not guarantee you a lifetime of happy and carefree sex, it will help you address painful or problematic aspects of your sexual story with courage, curiosity, and compassion. What would happen if we lived in a world that trusted, celebrated, protected, and supported female sexuality? Would half of all women in long-term relationships struggle with sexual desire problems? I have no idea. But the fact that women have a body part that exists solely for pleasure (yay clitoris!) suggests that we have quite a bit of untapped potential!

Reclaiming Your Sexy readies you for partnership with someone who can meet you in that self-aware space. Reclaiming Your Sexy also prepares you to raise the next generation of girls who can live from day one entitled to their voice, their boundaries, and their pleasure...and boys who are empathic and compassionate and who can be both tough and tender.

What You Won't Find in This Book

It's difficult to think of a topic that invites more opinion and judgment than the topic of sex, so here's what we are *not* going to do:

Bash men. I have so many men in my life whom I adore, and I hope you do as well. The problems we are unpacking are much bigger than blame. We need to work together, and we are inextricably bound: *Women's healing calls men forward, and men's accountability heals women.* In fact, chapter 12 is written for our male (and male-presenting) allies!

Apply rigid rules or use shame to create change. The goal is for you to determine—from the inside-out—how, when, where, why, and with whom you have sex.

Focus on "how to." This book is not explicitly about the mechanics of sex, but there are great how-to resources listed at the end of the book.

Create any expectation of what your relationship status is (or should be). Whether you are single, dating, engaged, married, or single again, you will find valuable tools and information.

"Should" all over ourselves. I have no expectation of whether, how, when, and with whom, you "should" be having sex. This book is about your relationship with your sexual self. Where you go from there is frankly none of my business!

What You Will Find in This Book

Sexualities are incredibly diverse. Readers of this book will have wildly different interests, desires, and relationship goals. This book strives only to support *your* deeper connection with *you* so you feel 100 percent empowered to author your unfolding story! On these pages, we will:

Name the problem. Women's sexual experiences are not as good, positive, rewarding, and pleasurable as they could be and should be.

Explore what gets in the way of healthy and pleasurable sexual experiences. We will look at how healthy sexual expression is constrained by inadequate sex education, sexism, inequitable distribution of power and privilege, dualistic (either-or) thinking, low-accountability and low-vulnerability hookup culture, family patterns, and a culture of sexual violence.

Encounter lots of shades of gray. There may not be fifty, but this book will invite you again and again to beware "the danger of the single story" as writer Chimamanda Ngozi Adichie says. We will resist easy answers, opting instead to trust that resilience grows by holding ever-more degrees of complexity. You will be asked to sit with paradoxes, points at which multiple things are all true: I am *both* courageous *and* afraid; I am *both* intrigued *and* intimidated by sex; I embody energy that is *both* feminine *and* masculine.

Grow your sexual self-awareness. Sexual self-awareness is a process of moving from an outside-in to an inside-out experience of Your Sexy.

Use an inclusive definition of sex. When people use the word "sex," they tend to mean a penis going into a vagina, but when I use the word "sex" in this book, I am referring to a big umbrella of erotic behaviors that may or may not include a penis going into a vagina. A big broad definition of what counts as sex fosters inclusion, imagination, permission, and pleasure.

Take an intersectional feminist approach. Heterosexual, gay, lesbian, bisexual, cisgender, gender queer, transgender, nonmonogamous, monogamous, and/or asexual, you belong on these pages. Your Sexy is you, as you are.

Apply and integrate. Throughout the book, you will find questions and exercises to help you with application and integration into your life. There are no right or wrong ways to approach these questions and exercises, but you might find it helpful to keep a journal near you as you read.

The Personal Is Political

One promise you must make with yourself as you begin this book is that you will never ever blame yourself for having developed an outside-in experience of Your Sexy. How could you be healthy in a wildly broken system? The vast majority of women have been the victims of some kind of violent harassment in public.[2] One-third of all women will be subjected to sexual violence in their lifetime, and the risk of sexual violence is higher for women of color and for those who belong to the LGBTQ+ community.[3] Our culture approaches sex in an *incredibly fragmented way*—obsessive and avoidant at the very same time. Hypersexualized images sell everything from cheeseburgers to eye shadow, while at the same time, parents (and teachers, religious leaders, and others in positions of authority) avoid talking about sex altogether or talk about it in fear-loaded and judgmental ways.

I believe we are living through a cultural transformation. Like so many people, I feel heartbroken by the inescapable awareness of the scope of women's suffering brought to light by the #MeToo movement.[4] But as my heart breaks, it also swells because the power of this movement is inspiring. This is a rising. A reckoning. A collective, "No more." This is women saying "no more" to sexual violence, certainly. But it is more than that. It is a "no more" to the shameful silence that has historically existed in the wake of sexual violence. Shameful silence that has allowed a culture of degradation to roll from generation to generation. What happens when stories move from the shadows of silence into the collective light of day? Transformation happens! What happens when women (and allies) stand together and say, "No more"? Space is made for "Yes!"

If women cannot say no, then women cannot truly say yes. When it comes to sex, that yes is essential. Sex requires a big, juicy, heartfelt, embodied yes. I believe that old ways are dying so new ways can be birthed. Transformation is destructive, uncomfortable, scary, and messy as hell. #MeToo is a movement of cultural and personal transformation, a movement that demands an end to sex as violence, sex as manipulation, and sex as power over. And it is a movement that holds the potential to create a culture of sex that is consensual, healing, and empowering.

Ending sexual violence requires change in lots of different domains (education, law, religion, public policy) and at multiple levels (individual, couple, family, community). We need to work together to make the world a place in which every sexual experience is one between consenting adults who cocreate the experience from start to finish. We must talk about women's bodies and struggles with sexual pleasure, not in a vacuum, but in a context. This book exists as one mere stone on a larger path that leads us away from lousy sexual experiences to wonderful ones.[5]

Our Declaration of Reclamation

I value the relationship between me and My Sexy. In some chapters of the story of my life, My Sexy will be a prominent, central, and vital feature, and in other chapters, My Sexy will be on hold. My Sexy is a part of me. It always has been and always will be, regardless of when, how, and with whom I express it. My Sexy is defined by me, and when I share My Sexy with others, my intention is that the experience is in the service of my health and well-being. I know that our culture has an incredibly problematic relationship with sex and that within this toxic framework, celebrating My Sexy is an ongoing and imperfect process, one that requires nothing short of fierce self-compassion. Shame blocks self-love, and the stories I carry about how My Sexy is dirty, sinful, wrong, and dangerous make it hard to live in flow with My Sexy. Naming these stories helps me bring them into the light of my awareness so I can ask, "To what degree does this story make me feel aligned and empowered versus ashamed and voiceless?" From that place of greater awareness, I let go of the stories that I never asked for and that do not serve me.

Coming Home to Ourselves

I want you to practice self-awareness as you read. Check in with yourself again and again. Notice when you find yourself *leaning in* to the material. Maybe you feel goosebumps, maybe tears well in your eyes, maybe you deeply sigh, or maybe you have a feeling of warmth inside of you. Those are moments in which you are letting go of an old way that wasn't serving you and inviting in something new that feels more nourishing. Notice too when you find yourself *feeling defensive* about the material. Maybe you feel like you want to say, "Yeah, but what about…" or maybe you feel queasy, ill-at-ease, angry. Those moments are invitations to dive a little deeper. Your resistance has much to teach you. I hope that the pages of this book help you find and listen to yourself, and I hope that this journey leaves you with the confidence and inspiration you need to create sexual experiences that serve you, heal you, and connect you—to yourself and to your intimate partners. Mostly I want you to integrate what feels valuable and resonant on these pages and leave behind what does not.

Before we dive in, it is important for me to locate myself. I am a woman. I am cisgender (meaning that my biological body and my gender identity align as female). I am white. I am an economically privileged Midwesterner. I come from a blended family that endured a variety of relational and emotional challenges that no doubt informed my decision to become a clinical psychologist. I am in midlife, in a long-term marriage, and the mother of two teens—a son and a daughter. I converted to Judaism and practice my spirituality in a big and wide way. You need to know this because even though I aspire to inclusivity, my writing cannot exist outside of my perspective, which has been forged through my experiences (professional and personal) and my identity.

You also should know that for years, I lived with a kind of internal split. I have always been nerdy...like homework-is-a-joy nerdy. I have also always been fascinated by sex. As kids, my friends and I loved to sneak our parents' copies of *The Joy of Sex* and sit in awe of the images. As a teen, I would look forward to Sunday nights because I would hide under the covers, crank up my Walkman, and listen to the radio show of the pioneering sex therapist Ruth Westheimer. But, for a long time, I was unsure how to reconcile these competing truths about myself. I felt like these two parts of me needed to remain very separate—the good girl and the bad girl. Through my personal and professional work, I have learned that I am far from alone. A lot of us experience a split between our erotic self and the rest of us. Knowing this has helped me feel entitled to honor and integrate My Sexy. This book is born from my inward journey, my reading and research, and my conversations with friends, clients, teachers, colleagues, and of course my intimate partner, Todd.

I am passionate about reclamation and integration of the sexual self. I am passionate about creating opportunities for people to shed shame and claim authenticity. I am passionate about helping people come home to themselves. Maybe someday this process won't be a reclamation. It will be the default. Maybe someday sex and relationship education will be wholehearted, preparing people to advocate for *both* safety *and* pleasure. Maybe someday all physical touch will begin with enthusiastic consent. Maybe someday there will be no sexual trauma, or at least, when it occurs, the victim will feel able to immediately speak up, be believed, and receive the care they need to recover, and the perpetrator will be held accountable. Maybe someday there will be no need to take sexy back because the sexual self will begin as, and remain, an integrated part of who we are. I hope each of us will do our part to create this world together.

Relational Self-Awareness 101

Self-awareness is the ability to take an honest look at your life without any attachment to it being right or wrong, good or bad.

—Debbie Ford, *The 21-Day Consciousness Cleanse*

The modern landscape of love and sex in so-called Western cultures includes degrees of freedom and complexity not available to the generations before you and still unavailable to people in other parts of the world. Intimate relationships have historically been role-bound contracts: he is the protector/hunter/breadwinner, and she is the caregiver/gatherer/domestic goddess. Whether the relationship was deemed to be a "good" one was determined by the degree to which each partner performed their assigned role. Our culture has shifted from role-to-role connection to soul-to-soul connection. We want our intimate partnerships to be vessels into which we can pour our deepest longings, yearning, and hopes. We expect more from our intimate partners than our ancestors could have ever dreamed of.

As a hopeless romantic, I have no issue with these elevated and expansive expectations, and I believe tirelessly and unapologetically in the power of love. Intimate relationships are the most powerful crucibles for growth and transformation available to us. But here's where the rubber hits the road for me. *If we are going to bring our hopes and dreams with us into our intimate relationships, we must also bring with us a perspective that allows us to view the challenges, pain points, and ebbs and flows as opportunities for personal growth and deepened intimacy.* The perspective we need for the high-wire act that is modern love is called *relational self-awareness*.

What Is Relational Self-Awareness?

Relational self-awareness is a paradigm that I have been working on throughout my career. It is the shift from looking for the "right person" to becoming the "right person." *Relational self-awareness is a curious and compassionate stance you take vis-à-vis yourself in which you view love as a classroom and yourself as a student, using the data of your thoughts, feelings, beliefs, and reactions to better understand who you are and what you need.* My first book, *Loving Bravely: Twenty Lessons of Self-Discovery to Help You Get the Love You Want,* posited that relational self-awareness is the cornerstone of a healthy romantic relationship. If you want a great romantic relationship with an intimate partner, you need a great relationship with YOU. How you relate to you sets the tone for the relationships you have with the people around you. Relational self-awareness is not a one-time self-knowledge learning process. It is a way of life. A paradigm shift.

Taking Sexy Back focuses on an aspect of relational self-awareness: *sexual self-awareness.* Sexual self-awareness is the process that moves you from an outside-in experience of your sexuality to an inside-out experience. Sexual self-awareness helps you to discern the internalized stories that serve you from the stories that do not. Sexual self-awareness moves you away from "shoulds" and toward an experience of yourself that is more authentic. We expand our sexual self-awareness by asking ourselves questions like:

- What were the early stories I was told about sex, and to what degree do they serve or hinder me today?

- What are the ingredients I need to have a "good" and fulfilling sexual experience with another person?

- What do I believe about the role of sex in an intimate relationship?

- What is my relationship with physical touch?

- How does my relationship with my body affect how I feel sexually?

- To what degree do I feel entitled to or deserving of pleasure?

You will ask yourself those questions and more as you move through the journey of this book.

Our Change Process: Name-Connect-Choose

In *Loving Bravely*, I introduced a three-step process designed to create change by expanding relational self-awareness: Name-Connect-Choose. Here, we will use the Name-Connect-Choose process to expand sexual self-awareness. Here's what it looks like:

Name. Tell your story, identify and declare something as your truth or your experience. Naming is powerful because it brings what was buried or out of your awareness into the light for examination.

Connect: Attune to yourself, turning your attention within and experiencing the emotions that are attached to the story you are telling. Connecting emotionally to your deep truth breathes life into your unearthed story.

Choose. Get curious about what else might be possible. Awareness facilitates choice. You now get to ask, "What do I choose for myself from this place of eyes-open empowerment?"

You will practice this process throughout the book as we explore a variety of issues, topics, and questions related to sexual self-awareness.

Sex Is Freaking Complicated

Shay, a woman I spoke with as I was writing this book, shared with me that for a long time, she felt repulsed by the idea of giving oral sex to a male partner. She judged herself as rigid and prudish for not wanting to go down on a guy, shaming herself for this "sexual hang-up." Shay experienced a big breakthrough in her sexual self-awareness as she began talking more openly with her female friends about sex. These conversations helped her let go of her story that she should be more sexually open-minded and chill and normalized that having a complicated relationship with sex is, well, normal! A big aha for her was unpacking how the intersection of race, gender, and sex lives within her. As an African American woman, kneeling before a man felt to her like an enactment racist tropes about black women as "sex-obsessed Jezebels or video vixens who perform for men's pleasure."

Through these conversations, Shay has begun to move from an outside-in relationship to Her Sexy to a relationship that is more inside-out, and her process can be mapped onto the Name-Connect-Choose trajectory. She *named* this connection between sex, gender, and race, which gave her much-needed clarity about her sexual block. She *connected* emotionally, allowing herself to feel both anger at our culture and compassion for herself. She now feels better able to *choose* what feels authentic to her, and what she has found is that when she can talk with a partner who is ready, willing, and able to unpack the complexities of race, gender, and sex with her, the very same act feels empowering and fun.

One major takeaway from Shay's story? Thank the goddesses for sex talk with friends! Our friends have the power to listen us into clarity, and wholehearted conversations help us offload shame big time. My team and I wrote a reader's guide, called *The Sexy in Me Honors the Sexy in You*, which you can find, along with a few other resources, at http://www.newharbinger.com/33461, to get you and your squad started. The other takeaway from Shay's story is that sex is freaking complicated. Your Sexy contains mystery, history, and paradox. Your Sexy is:

- *dynamic*, developing and changing over time

- *embedded*, traveling with you into the various domains of your life (work, school, friendships, romantic relationships)

- *intersectional*, informed by your cultural contexts of membership, like race, ethnicity, gender identity, sexual orientation, religious affiliation, socioeconomic status, age, and geography[6]

- *embodied*, affected by and affecting you as a physical being.

Sex can be hard to talk about, in part because the topic touches every aspect of the human experience. But we can't talk about everything at once. What seems to happen is that the moment one aspect of sex is highlighted (the biology of sex, for example), what rushes to the foreground for people is everything *not* being highlighted, like the psychology of sex, or the politics of sex, or the ethics of sex. And when one aspect is more relevant for someone, they feel misunderstood or diminished by those people for whom a different aspect is more relevant. And that space of difference becomes a space of misunderstanding, so we retreat from conversations we need to be having. *It is precisely within conversations that we learn how to hold the degrees of complexity that Our Sexy deserves.*

The Map of Sexual Self-Awareness

Legendary sex therapist Esther Perel describes sex as "a place you go."[7] If sex is a place you go, then you're gonna need a map so you don't get lost. I want to introduce you to the map I developed. All the professional work I do is informed by an approach called integrative systemic therapy (IST).[8] We're not going to get technical about IST because we have other business that needs our attention, so I'll just say that IST therapists and thinkers believe that the problems we face in our lives are complicated and require us to use a variety of tools to understand and shift what feels painful and confusing. And that IST perspective inspired the "Map of Sexual Self-Awareness" (shown in the figure below). *The Map of Sexual Self-Awareness illuminates seven aspects of sex and provides the framework we will use to guide the curious and compassionate exploration of Your Sexy.*

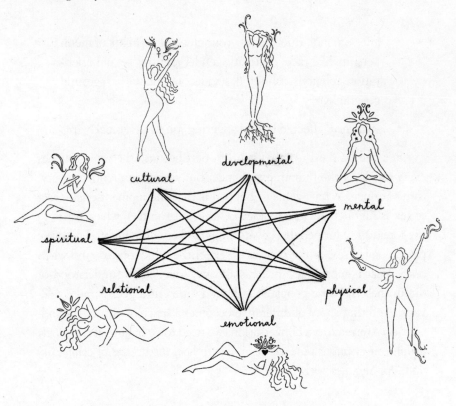

The Map of Sexual Self-Awareness

We will visit each of these seven aspects in part 2 of the book in order to deepen your relationship with Your Sexy. Here's an overview of each aspect, followed by questions you can reflect on in your journal.

Cultural

Your Sexy is embedded in a larger cultural context, and you have spent years absorbing highly gendered stories about who you *should be* sexually. These stories are ubiquitous and sneaky. Bringing them into the light of day for examination frees you up to make conscious choices versus kneejerk responses governed by cultural conditioning.

Developmental

Who you were sexually as a teen is different from who you are sexually today, and who you are sexually today is different from who you will be ten and twenty years from now. The sex we have changes—in terms of why we have it, how it feels, and what it means.

Mental

Your brain is your biggest sex organ. The thoughts you have about sex shape Your Sexy and affect the sex that you have. Mindfulness and self-compassion are powerful and well-researched pathways toward more wholehearted sexual experiences.

Physical

Sex is an embodied experience, so the relationship you have with this flesh and blood carrier of your soul—your body—shapes your sexual experiences. The more you know, understand, and appreciate your body, the more you can enjoy the pleasures of sex.

Emotional

Our culture tends to hold the world of feelings in disdain, associating emotions with weakness, yet, when it comes to sex, vulnerability is 100 percent unavoidable. All emotions—good, bad, and ugly—are data. Painful experiences leave imprints that shape how you experience your sexuality, but healing is always possible.

Relational

Most sex takes place between people.[9] Sex is an experience of relating to another—a dance that requires communication and collaboration and yields connection and closeness.

Spiritual

Spirituality is that deeply personal and unique relationship between our human self and the divine. Spiritual practices and beliefs can enhance or constrain our ability to experience sexual pleasure, empowerment, and connection. Sex can be a profoundly spiritual experience with the potential to move us toward greater compassion and awareness.

Cultural

- What are the main stories I have internalized from my culture about who I should be sexually?

- How do those stories enhance or compromise my sexual experiences?

Developmental

- As a teen, My Sexy was…

- Right now, My Sexy is…

- In the future, I hope My Sexy will be…

Mental

- What are the thoughts and beliefs I carry about My Sexy?

- How do my thoughts enhance (or detract from) my experiences of sex?

Physical

- What is the quality of my relationship with my body, including my genitals?

- How does my relationship with my body enhance or constrain my sexual experiences?

Emotional

- How do I tend to feel before, during, and after sex? What are the emotions that I *would like to* associate with my sexual experiences?

- To what degree do painful experiences from my past shape My Sexy today?

Relational

- What do I believe is the role of sex in an intimate relationship?

- To what degree is sex a source of pleasure and play in my intimate relationships? To what degree is sex a source of stress and conflict in my intimate relationships?

Spiritual

- To what degree does my relationship with God, oneness, higher power, or spirit enhance my experience of My Sexy?

- To what degree does my relationship with God, oneness, higher power, or spirit constrain my experience of My Sexy?

Make Love Not Fear

As you look at the Map of Sexual Self-Awareness, notice that the word *love* appears nowhere, begging the question, *What's the relationship between love and sex?* You probably have been given answers to that question in your life: perhaps you were taught that you should only have sex with someone you love, or perhaps you were taught that having sex with someone will make you fall in love with them (or make them fall in love with you). Although we've established that I'm not invested in dictating a set of sexual rules, I would like to challenge you to consider this idea: *love ought to always accompany sex.* Bear with me! I want to break this down.

One of my favorite spiritual teachers, Neale Donald Walsch, says, "There are only two energies at the core of the human experience: love and fear."[10] All of our choices, including our sexual choices, are guided by fear or love. Sexual experiences that are guided by fear sound like this: *I will be rejected or abandoned if we don't have sex. Something is wrong with me/us if we don't have sex. I can't have sex, otherwise people will think I'm a slut.* Sexual experiences that are fueled by love sound simply like this: *Yes.*

Your alignment with and your connection to Your Sexy helps you feel the difference between fear and love. Your celebration of Your Sexy as wise, beautiful, sacred, and yours makes it so the only kind of sex that makes sense anymore is love-infused sex. The journey through this book will make it easier for you to discern between the energy of love and the energy of fear. When you notice that fear is taking the wheel and beginning to guide your decision making, you can say no and hold a boundary authentically and unapologetically. And, when you know and feel that love is in the driver's seat, you can say yes in a way that is turned-on, empowered, and joyful.

A graduate student of mine shared a story that captures this distinction between fear and love. She was studying late one night when a guy she was hooking up with texted her to meet up for sex. Her kneejerk reaction was that if he was reaching out, she needed to meet up. But just as she was getting ready to respond to his text, she caught a glimpse of the *Loving Bravely* book out of the corner of her eye, and she remembered the importance of pausing and checking in with herself. So instead of responding to his text right away, she closed her eyes and did a brief Name-Connect-Choose Process.

Name. The guy I'm hooking up with wants to meet up with me for sex.

Connect. I can feel the tug of fear that if I don't go and have sex with him, he will feel critical and disappointed. He might even move on and find someone else. I can also feel the tug of a crystal clear "no" in my body. I really do not feel available to have sex with him tonight.

Choose. I give myself permission to say no, and I give him permission to feel however he wants to feel about my choice.

By pausing and checking in with herself, her deep truth revealed itself right away. She did not feel like having sex with him that night, and her kneejerk urge to say yes to his request was guided by a *fear* of being abandoned.

Saying yes because you are afraid of the consequences that might accompany your no, that's the energy of fear. Saying yes because you want to say yes, that's the energy of love. Saying no because you're afraid of how you'll be perceived if you say yes, that's the energy of fear. Saying no because you checked in with yourself and that choice isn't aligned with who you are or who you want to be, that's the energy of love. In moments of choice, pause and check in with yourself. Learn how the energy of love and the energy of fear feel inside of your body. Cultivate relationships that are rich with heartfelt yeses and loving nos.

The Golden Equation of Love

When you commit to practicing sexual and relational self-awareness, you are committing to a more complicated view of the world. You are committing to considering, again and again, the ways in which your thoughts, feelings, and behaviors shape (and are shaped by) your context. *It doesn't matter whether we are talking about a first date, a casual sexual encounter, or a couple in their twentieth year of marriage; an intimate relationship is a system.* What you do affects your partner, and what your partner does affects you. Back and forth, round and round, we cue off each other again and again. This is a harder, and better, way to relate to love.

You see, when you choose a partner, you choose a particular relational dance. The choreography of that dance is built upon the "stuff" that each of you brings into the relationship. It's 100 percent unavoidable to bring stuff into a relationship. Each of you has a profile of personality traits, strengths, and weaknesses. And each of you has a history that is rich with heartbreaks and victories that have shaped how you "do" intimate relationships. You both are profoundly imperfect and forever-evolving human beings.

The research is clear. Conflict is inevitable, so our best and bravest work is to manage our differences with grace, humility, and collaboration.[11] Love, by its very nature, is triggering. Romantic love cracks us wide open, which is both exciting and terrifying at the same time. Falling in love, creating emotional intimacy and trust, and cultivating sexual intimacy make us feel vulnerable. Your challenge is to stay open to, curious about, and responsible for all the ways that love stirs you. That's a lot easier to do when you can remember that it's okay to be stirred up by the challenges inherent in loving and being loved. The more we can humbly take responsibility for our stuff, the more we can ask our partners to be patient and kind as we try to figure it out.

One of my favorite relational self-awareness tools is *the Golden Equation of Love.* Every relational interaction can be mapped onto this equation:

MY STUFF + YOUR STUFF = OUR STUFF

My *stuff* is made up of my quirks, peccadillos, old wounds, traumas, hang-ups, patterns, and preferences. *Your stuff* is made up of your quirks, peccadillos, old wounds, traumas, hang-ups, patterns, and preferences. *Our stuff* is the unique dance that occurs when my stuff and your stuff comingle. The happiest and healthiest intimate relationships are made up of two people who are committed to honoring the Golden Equation of Love by curiously and compassionately exploring again and again what's happening within and between them.

Here's an example of the Golden Equation of Love in action. My client Lucy barely smiled at me as she sat down for our usual Tuesday session. When I asked her how she was doing, she launched into the story of a first date gone awry. She and Tal spent a wonderful afternoon and evening together. Adventurous and playful by nature, she loved that they had gone for a long walk and played board games at a neighborhood bar. When Tal asked her to come back to her place to listen to music, Lucy told her that she was interested in hanging out longer but wanted to go slow sexually. Tal shared that she was on the same page. Back at Tal's place, they talked, flirted, and enjoyed a passionate make-out session. As they were kissing, Lucy asked her if she wanted a hickey. Tal said yes. She gave her a hickey. It was quite late, and Lucy decided to spend the night.

The next morning, they woke up slowly and were chatting and snuggling when Tal's hickey caught Lucy's eye. "Oh my gosh," Lucy exclaimed. "Your hickey is so big!" Tal jumped up to look in the mirror, and she started to panic. "Shit! Shit! Shit!" she yelled. She grabbed her phone and started to Google how to get rid of a hickey. Lucy tried to offer support, but Tal was spiraling. Unsure and embarrassed, Lucy apologized to Tal, gave her a hug, and headed out. Later that day, Lucy texted her to find out how she was doing and to follow up on some plans they had talked about the night before. Tal sent her a one-line reply, and the connection soon fizzled. Lucy felt frustrated and so embarrassed. "I just feel like I'm too much," she lamented to me.

Lucy's story was shame-filled. She felt like she screwed up their budding connection with her bold sexuality. *Stories that are shame-filled, or blame-filled, are stories that are not honoring the Golden Equation of Love.* In session, I invited her to consider that when Tal slowly faded out of Lucy's life, it was because something was going on for Tal as well. Maybe she felt disappointed in herself that she had gotten so lost in a sexual moment. Maybe she felt embarrassed that Lucy saw her have a big emotional reaction. We don't know. What we do know is that without access to Tal's story, Lucy was left telling a story that her stuff ruined them. Lucy, in her shame-filled place, hadn't even considered what might have been happening for Tal, and the Golden Equation of Love offered her some much-needed relief from her self-critical story. With this more relationally self-aware perspective, she could consider what she wanted to learn from this experience from a place of compassion, not shame.

Love and sex put us in touch with powerful and ancient magic. What gets stirred is deep and confusing and can make you feel seriously vulnerable. Practicing relational self-awareness will help you make sense of what you're thinking and feeling. The goal isn't to feel less but rather to trust yourself to be resilient in the face of love's never-ending pulls.

❋

Sexual and relational self-awareness are about understanding your relationship to relationships. An ongoing commitment to taking a curious and compassionate stance vis-à-vis yourself creates the foundation for a happy and healthy intimate relationship…and great sex!

3

Of Warts, Bananas, and Birth Videos

My silences had not protected me. Your silence will not protect you.

—Audre Lorde, *Your Silence Will Not Protect You*

Looking back helps us grow. By naming the stories we internalized early in our lives and examining the imprint those stories made, we chart a course for our evolution. And when it comes to the early messages we got about sex, most of us are in desperate need of some transformation! A student said to me recently, "Throughout my childhood and adolescence, I never learned about sex without also learning about diseases. Those two things feel permanently merged inside my brain."

Think back to the sex education you received in junior high and high school—if you received any sex education at all. What stands out in your memory? The condom on the banana? The miracle of birth video? The close-up photos of genitalia ravaged by sexually transmitted infections (STIs)? If you went to college, did you receive any additional sex education? For those whose sex education included an *object lesson*, this likely made a large impression.

A graduate student of mine remembers his object lesson clearly though it happened almost a decade ago. His teacher passed around a length of scotch tape. Each student pressed the tape against their forearm and then passed it on to the student next to them. When the tape was handed back to the teacher, it was rather gross and had lost its stickiness, and the teacher explained that the same thing happens with sex: having multiple sexual partners impairs your ability to have a healthy relationship because you've lost your ability to bond (stick) to a partner. After I picked my jaw up off the floor, I asked my student about the impact that object lesson had on him, and he shared, "For me, it embedded the shame-driven narrative that sex lowers your value as a human being and reinforced the notion that the sexual bond is painful and decreases your worth with each subsequent lover other than your first. As a gay man, since same-sex intercourse was never discussed, I made the assumption and internalized the belief that silence equals disgust and taboo."[12]

Of course, we need to teach young people about reproduction, the biology of sex, and how to prevent STIs, unwanted pregnancy, and sexual assault, but ask yourself: "What is the impact of a sex ed curriculum that focuses heavily on risk and danger, emphasizing what not to do? What is left unspoken, and what do those omissions convey?"

Adrienne, a twenty-four-year-old woman, shared with me some reflections on what it was like to learn about sex in her religiously conservative school system. "Before middle school, the boys and girls were separated in order to educate us about how our bodies were changing. The girls were taught about their periods and how it is important to make babies, while the boys were taught about erections and ejaculation. Sex as a concept wasn't introduced until ninth grade, but in the form of consequences. I remember our teacher giving us condoms to carry with us at all times, but the culture among the students really viewed sex as shameful and carrying condoms meant they were engaging in something they were not supposed to be doing."

How helpful that Adrienne's school provided her with information and even condoms! This is more than some people receive for sure. But by separating students by gender, schools limit access to information and reinforce the idea that guys and girls shouldn't be interacting anywhere near anything sexual. In addition, this separation reinforces the notion that gender is binary and renders invisible the experiences of LGBTQ+ youth. What's the impact of not teaching girls about erections and ejaculation? What's the impact of not teaching boys about pregnancy and periods? What's the impact of waiting until puberty to talk about sex?

Every generation needs to figure out how to talk with the next generation about sex. The topic of "The Talk" fascinates me because it captures so much all at once—culture, gender, family dynamics, and sex![13] *The intention of this chapter is to help you understand the impact of the choices made on your behalf about how you should be educated about sex.* The messages you were given by the generation above you is your inheritance. What you impart to the next generation is your legacy. By understanding our inheritance, we can choose with eyes wide open what we want our legacy to be.

> Write responsively to these questions:
>
> • Who taught you about sex?
>
> • Would you describe your sex education as more steeped in *fear* or more steeped in *love*?
>
> • What messages did you receive about how you should act sexually? How do you feel about those messages today?

The Power of the Unspoken

A sex therapist I consulted with on this book told me a story about how schools and parents perpetuate silence regarding sex. A fourth-grade student asked his school counselor, "Where do babies come from?" and the counselor's response was, "That's something you should ask your parents." Deflated, the kid responded, "They told me to ask you." When schools think it's family's job and family thinks it's school's job, the silences become deafening.

Researchers from Harvard surveyed more than three thousand men and women ages eighteen to twenty-five, and they found that 70 percent of them wished that their parents had talked with them about relationships and 65 percent of them wished they had relationship education at school.[14] Likely, your family offered you more silence than dialog, and you had to turn elsewhere. In my day, that meant hunting down a parent's stash of *Hustler* magazines or *The Joy of Sex* book. Today that means diving into the world of free streaming porn, little of which is intended to serve as sex education and which can leave one with some rather skewed (and scary) notions about sex.

When sex is shrouded in silence, it's easy to equate being curious with being bad, dirty, sinful, and, God-forbid, slutty. Adrienne, whose story we heard earlier in the chapter, explained it to me like this: "Late-night HBO, Cinemax, and the Internet taught me about sex. As a curious middle-schooler looking for answers, these were the only 'safe' options (so as to not be looked upon as a bad person or a sexual deviant)." *Sexual curiosity is normal.* Adrienne wasn't saying she wanted to have sex. She wanted to have knowledge about sex. Those are not the same thing.

When adults do not feel ready (or authorized) to meet kids' sexual curiosity with compassion and information, kids end up feeling very ashamed about their very normal curiosity. But how can adults meet kids' sexual curiosity with compassion and information, given that when those adults were kids, the adults around *them* didn't know how to meet *their* curiosity with compassion and information? It's time to break the cycle, don't you think? The cycle gets broken when sex education is guided by love instead of fear.

- When fear guides sex education, the belief is that normalizing sexuality in any way, shape, or form is tantamount to condoning wild and reckless sexual behavior. When love guides sex education, kids get the message that curiosity about sex and readiness for sex are *not* the same thing.

- When fear guides sex education, LGBTQ+ sexualities are omitted, sending the message that LGBTQ+ sexualities are deviant. When love guides sex education, LGBTQ+ sexualities are integrated, sending the message to queer and straight students alike that everyone belongs and has worth.

- When fear guides sex education, porn isn't talked about. When love guides sex education, young people are provided with the information they need to make healthy and safe choices regarding the reality that we live in a world with readily available porn.

Silence carries weight, contains meaning, and creates a vacuum that shame fills in. Your Sexy is desperate for you to unpack your inheritance—the messages you've been handed about sex and touch, including both the spoken and the avoided, from the outside-in, from your schools, your religious institutions, and your family. It's time to carry forth that which serves Your Sexy and give back that which fuels a sense that Your Sexy is bad, dirty, or wrong.

Write responsively to the following questions:

- How did your family talk about touch (nonsexual touch and sexual touch)? What were the messages you internalized about touching and being touched?

- How much touch/closeness/affection was there in your family as you were growing up? How does that shape how you "do" love today?

- What were the words used to describe genitals? To describe sex? What did those language choices convey to you about bodies and sexuality?

Is This the Whole Story?

Deep political and social divides underlie the debate about how young people should be educated about sex. Sex education curricula are created by a variety of stakeholders including religious groups, hospital staff, and youth advocacy groups and can be broadly divided into two categories: abstinence-only-until-marriage (AOUM) curricula and comprehensive curricula. Since 1981, the federal government has spent over $2 billion on abstinence-only sex education, but when researchers study the impact of these programs, here's what's crystal clear: AOUM curricula don't work.

These programs do not reduce teen pregnancy rates, and teens who receive abstinence-based sex education are not more likely to abstain from sex than teens who receive comprehensive sex education.

In fact, these two groups of teens have similar numbers of sexual partners and become sexually active at around the same age.[15] Further teens who receive abstinence-only sex education and/or who take purity are less likely to use protection when they do have sex.[16] This makes sense. If you believe that your choice to have sex makes you bad/slutty/sinful, the conditions are ripe for enormous shame—shame that can keep you from taking steps to protect yourself.

Comprehensive sex education programs do teach abstinence as one way to prevent STIs, unplanned pregnancy, and the emotional and relational complexities that accompany sex…just not the *only* way. As sex educator Eric Sprankle said, "A sex-ed class that only focuses on STIs is like a wood shop class that only focuses on table saw injuries."[17] Under the Obama administration, federal funding shifted toward comprehensive sex education, and the shift was beginning to pay off. Birth rates among teens ages fifteen to nineteen dropped by half between 2007 to 2017.[18] Nevertheless, the Trump Administration has not prioritized comprehensive sex education, and, in July 2017, it pulled more than $200 million of funding for comprehensive, evidence-based sex education programs designed to reduce teen pregnancy.[19]

Chances are good that your sex education didn't provide you with what you need. A study found that less than 50 percent of the high schools and fewer than 20 percent of the middle schools in America covered all sixteen topics that the Centers for Disease Control have determined constitute an adequate sex education.[20] Data from 2011 to 2013 indicate that "43 percent of adolescent females and 57 percent of adolescent males did not receive information about birth control before they had sex for the first time."[21] Although comprehensive sex education is better than the alternative, it is still inadequate because it omits key topics like porn literacy, masturbation, body image, pleasure, and how to talk with a partner about sex. Given all of this, we must commit ourselves to continuing sex education.

Becoming Sex Positive

Sex positivity is an ideology that "promotes, with respect to gender and sexuality, being open-minded, nonjudgmental, and respectful of personal sexual autonomy, when there is consent."[22] Here's a sweet example of sex positivity in action. A friend of mine who is a sex educator was explaining to her young daughter where babies come from. She said, "When two people want to make a baby, they get naked together, and they do a special hug." Her daughter asked the logical next question, "But mom, what if the man's penis accidentally touches the woman's vagina?" Not missing a beat, Mama replied, "If you really love the other person, you don't mind so much. In fact, it feels good." Her daughter's response? "Oh."

What might be different if we commit to cultivating sex-positivity? If we insist that sex is a normal, natural, and pleasurable part of life? If we say unequivocally that sexualities are wildly and wonderfully diverse and that we have a lifetime to define and refine our own? That gender is far from binary?[23] That masturbation is not only not a sin but also a safe and healthy way to get to know your body? What might happen if each one of us believed that we are entitled to sexual experiences that serve us, body, heart, and soul?

Your Sexy implores you to do two things: grieve the education you needed but didn't receive *and* authorize yourself to become a lifelong learner about sex. It is time for you to embrace a sex positive approach to sexual health.

The journey to sex positivity is a journey from fear to love. Identifying as sex positive says absolutely nothing about how Your Sexy is expressing herself in the world. You can identify as sex positive while practicing abstinence or while having lots of sex. You can identify as sex positive while enjoying "vanilla" sex or kinky sex. You can identify as sex positive while engaging in sexual monogamy or consensual nonmonogamy (CNM).[24] Being sex positive is an attitude—one that we practice in order to shed shame we didn't ask for so we might cultivate self-acceptance and grace instead.

Pleasure Principles

As we wrap this chapter up, let's return to Adrienne's story. Although she grew up feeling disempowered and disconnected from Her Sexy, she is building a wonderful relationship with a man who cares deeply about her...and her sexual pleasure. She shared with me, "I recently read *She Comes First* by Ian Kerner, and I had never once conceptualized that sex should be thoroughly enjoyed by both parties, rather than a performance put on by one person (her) that the other person enjoys. It sounds terrible, but I think a lot of women lie to themselves about enjoying sex because they hear or see that it should be enjoyable, and if it's not, something is wrong with them."

Adrienne is naming the logical consequence of inadequate sex education—the nearly ubiquitous tendency for women to fake orgasms. We will come back to this later in the book to seek both understanding and remedy. Adrienne's journey to take Her Sexy back currently centers on discovering pleasure. She has authorized herself to become a lifelong learner by reading about women's pleasure, which has helped her shift from *sex as performance* to *sex as expression*. Her empowerment mixed with her partner's attunement creates the opening for her to experience the pleasure that nobody had told her she deserves. As we enter part 2, it is time now for your journey to begin.

❊

Every culture needs to figure out how to educate its next generation about sex, but it's likely that your sex education left a lot to be desired. Your clarity about how you learned about sex and the degree to which it served (and didn't serve) Your Sexy is an essential aspect of sexual self-awareness. How amazing that we get to be lifelong learners and that we can shed fear and shame by continuing to educate ourselves about sex.

PART II

The Journey to Sexual Self-Awareness

cultural

Living and Loving
in a Patriarchy

The same sexist narratives that suggest a woman's worth lies in her
sexual desirability suggest a man's worth lies in his strength—and
disregards those who identify outside the gender binary altogether.
Culturally entrenched beliefs like these dictate the characteristics
one must embody or face the threat of marginalization and
violence.

—Kristen J Sollee, *Witches, Sluts, Feminists*

The first section of this chapter may read like a Gender Studies 101
lecture, but I am going to need you to hang in there with me for a hot
minute. We are going to look at how *the personal is political* because
this old-school slogan from 1960s feminism is super relevant to your
sexual self-awareness journey. By expanding your awareness about how
power and *privilege* operate in our culture at the broadest level, you
create new possibilities for your relationship with Your Sexy, and you
invite wonderful, rewarding, and enriching ways to express Your Sexy.
Deep breath, my love, let's do this!

All Oppression Is Connected

We live in a wildly diverse world. Humanity takes so many forms.
People are:

- young and old and in between

- able and disabled and in between

- wealthy and poor and in between

- male, female, gender fluid, nonbinary, and beyond

- gay, straight, bisexual, queer, and so many more

- Christian, Jewish, Muslim, atheist, agnostic, and so many more.

But, by and large, our culture has struggled to:

- live with fascination and curiosity about the diversity of humanity

- embrace how diversity enhances our lives by offering us a richer range of perspectives, connections, and opportunities

- work collectively to ensure that everyone has access to what they need to survive and thrive.

Instead, from *differences*, we have created *hierarchies*. "These people" are inherently better than "those people," or "these ways of being human" are inherently better than "those ways of being human." Once a hierarchy has been established, it is far easier to justify inequities of power, privilege, and access by saying that those with more power have it because they are better/stronger/faster/harder-working, and those with less power are in that spot because they are "less than." So that we can figure out how to live and love in a patriarchy, let's define some terms.

"Patriarchy" is a social system that values masculinity over femininity, in which men are privileged in relation to women, dominant over women, and granted greater access to power. It is one of those hierarchies that has been persistent and pernicious for thousands of years. A patriarchal system perpetuates a gender binary by attempting to reduce gender diversity into one of two boxes—a male box and a female box (more on that in a bit). Patriarchy hurts people of *all genders* by limiting everyone's access to the full spectrum of human experience. All of us are prevented from living in a wholehearted way because we are granted or denied access to experiences and emotions based solely on our biological sex. Men are taught to split off, suppress, and deny any aspect of themselves that could be considered feminine so they can be men in the "right" way, and women are taught to split off, suppress, and deny any aspect of themselves that could be considered masculine so they can be women in the "right" way. The consequences for breaking these gendered rules can be anything from invisibility to bullying, marginalization, violence, and even murder.

"Feminism" is, broadly defined, the sociological pushback against patriarchy—a social movement that seeks to improve the lives of women and men by redistributing value, power, and privilege between the sexes in the service of greater equality. The history of the feminist movement, especially in the United States, is *both* impressive *and* fraught! The range of choices available to women today, in both our public and private lives, is the product of generations of courage, activism, and resistance. At the very same time, the feminist movement has been appropriately criticized for focusing on the experiences of sexism in the lives of white, cisgender, middle-class, and able-bodied women, marginalizing and silencing the voices of women of color, members of the queer community, poor women, and women who live with disabilities.

"Intersectional feminism," a term coined in 1989 by feminist theorist Kimberlé Crenshaw, provides an inclusive path forward. Crenshaw defines intersectional feminism as, "The view that women experience oppression in varying configurations and in varying degrees of intensity. Cultural patterns of oppression are not only interrelated but are bound together and influenced by the intersectional systems of society. Examples of this include race, gender, class, ability, and ethnicity."[25] In other words, gender is a vital aspect of identity, but it is not the only aspect of identity. All forms of oppression are connected, so efforts to transform systems of power and privilege must be inclusive—committed to studying how race, ethnicity, socioeconomic status, religion, sexuality, and ability profoundly shape one's experience of gender. As Audre Lorde said, "There is no such thing as a single-issue struggle because we do not live single-issue lives."[26]

The fight to transform gender inequities happens at the level of large institutional systems like education, health care, and criminal justice. And gender inequalities happen at the level of small systems, like intimate relationships. "Intimate justice" is a term introduced by gender studies professor Sara McClelland to bridge the big macro-sociopolitical world and the little micro-world of a sexual encounter between individuals. Intimate justice is "a theoretical framework that links experiences of inequity in the sociopolitical domain with how individuals imagine and evaluate the quality of their sexual and relational experiences."[27]

Your position within larger social hierarchies shapes what you feel you are entitled to because we bring our whole selves into the bedroom with us. If you've been given the message, in large and small ways, that you matter less than other people, it may be foreign for you to feel that your body belongs to you and you alone or to feel authorized to advocate for your needs for safety, comfort, respect, and pleasure. The fact that we live in a world of profound intimate injustices is tragic, and I want you to feel fully entitled to all the grief and rage this stirs in you. Just promise to meet those strong emotions with your boundless self-compassion.

Here's an example of how couples navigate identity, power, and privilege in the bedroom. Erin and Tyler have been dating for a year. Both are conservative Christians who are committed to abstaining from penetrative sex until they are married. In the meantime, Tyler is interested in kissing Erin while lying in bed in just their underwear, but Erin feels that is outside of the boundaries of what their faith permits. They talk collaboratively and openly about how to bridge this difference, and each has a lot of empathy for the other's perspective. And, at the same time, Erin is aware that there are power differences woven into their relationship that subtly influence their conversation. Erin is an Asian American woman who has internalized the message again and again that she is valued for the degree to which she accommodates the needs of others, especially men. Tyler is a white man who has received a very different message about what he is entitled to ask for.

Erin is definitely turned on by Tyler's fantasy, and she feels he's asking from a place of love, not manipulation. But she wants some time and space to listen to herself from within. If she is going to make the choice to expand her sexual boundaries in the ways that Tyler is inviting them to do, she wants to do so from a place of feeling *both* connected to her own desire *and* at peace with her relationship to her faith. She feels the urge to say yes to Tyler's request to make him happy, but she anticipates that a quick yes would feel like a replication of the script she has internalized her whole life—that Asian American women need to be submissive and pleasing. How might this process of sexual decision-making have looked if the partner with *less* culturally ascribed power (in terms of gender and race) had been the one asking for a *more* relaxed sexual boundary?

The purpose of considering how identities like race and gender affect what we feel able to ask for, or decline, in the bedroom isn't to make people feel guilty about who they are. Rather it is to appreciate the context in which all sexual decision-making happens so our choices feel empowered and aligned!

More Boxes, Please

Each of us exists as the coming together of many identity variables, yet the pressure to reduce ourselves to either "this" or "that" can feel crushing. Gender is a great example of this. Our culture has attempted to put all of humanity into one of two boxes based solely on whether you're the owner of a penis or a vagina. Reality ends up being more complicated because gender is about more than biological sex. My favorite tool for helping people create a more nuanced story about their gendered selves is called the Genderbread Person.[28] Created by activist Sam Killermann, the Genderbread Person is a diagram that allows you to locate yourself along five gender-related dimensions.

Working on this diagram is a favorite for my students because it gives them the opportunity to expand the vocabulary they use about their gendered self. Naming is so empowering! And naming is the first step toward connecting with the feelings you carry about your gendered self—for example, shame about ways in which you might not fit neatly within the male box or the female box. The five dimensions are *gender identity, gender expression, biological sex, sexual attraction,* and *romantic attraction.* These five dimensions are independent of each other and may also change over time for you.

Gender identity. Gender identity is how you think about yourself in terms of your gender. Historically we have used two boxes—man or woman (or boy or girl). Maybe you fit perfectly in one of those boxes in terms of how you think about yourself. Maybe not. The gender identity of some folks is far from binary, and they may use a term like "gender expansive" or "genderqueer" to capture how they live beyond the binary.

Gender expression. Gender expression is how you manifest or display your gender in your dress, voice, behavior, mannerisms, and so forth. Whether we like it or not, much of the world is coded in masculine and feminine terms. In a Western cultural context, long hair, makeup, and skirts are associated with feminine gender expression, and short hair and neckties are associated with masculine gender expression. How you "show up" and are "read" by others is your gender expression.

Biological sex. Biological sex is about what's "under the hood" as Killermann says. It's about hormones, genetics, genitalia, and other secondary sexual characteristics. Options here include being a man, a woman, or intersex. Intersex means that your body is not strictly male or female. About 1 percent of people live in bodies that are neither "standard" female nor "standard" male.[29]

Sexual attraction. Sexual attraction is about the direction of your erotic attraction. The spectrum here runs from men/males/masculinity to women/females/femininity. The focus here is on the physical.

Romantic attraction. Romantic attraction is a little broader and is about the direction of your romantic and relational attraction. With whom would you like to build a romantic relationship? The spectrum here runs from men/males/masculinity to women/females/femininity. The focus here is on the emotional.

The complexity of gender is why I feel a bit cringy about gender reveal parties. You know the deal. The expecting couple heads to the OBGYN for the twenty-week ultrasound. The results are placed in a hermetically sealed envelope and taken to the local party supply store. There, the clerk fills a box with either blue balloons or pink balloons and seals it up tight! The couple gathers family and friends. The box is opened. The big secret is revealed.

I hate to be a (gender reveal) party pooper, but here are the two issues I have with this craze. First, it's not a gender reveal party; it's a biological sex reveal party. The parents have learned whether there's a teeny weenie or a lil' v-jay-jay. That's it! They know nothing of this being's internal experience of self! Second, these parties highlight and reinforce all the expectations we project onto little beings, even before they have come into this world. Gender reveal party themes you can find on Pinterest include "guns or glitter," "staches or lashes," "lures or lace," and "cupcake or stud muffin." Can we cool it already with the promotion of the gender binary? Rant over.

Pinterest pet peeve aside, I feel so inspired by the ways in which the world is becoming ever-more willing to move beyond the two-box mode. For example, on the dating app OkCupid, users can identify themselves using up to five of these options: woman, man, agender, androgynous, bigender, cis man, cis woman, genderfluid, genderqueer, gender nonconforming, hijra, intersex, non-binary, other, pangender, transfeminine, transgender, transmasculine, transsexual, trans man, trans woman, and two-spirit. Naming where you "live" on these dimensions grants Your Sexy the freedom to be glorious and complicated and worthy of loving and being loved.

Take a look at the Genderbread Person, which is available online at http://www.newharbinger.com/33461, and see where you'd place yourself on the five continua. Reflect on whether any of the continua felt especially challenging or emotionally evocative to you and why that might be.

Being Both Powerful and Connected

One of my favorite therapy gurus, Terry Real, says, "In a patriarchy, you can be powerful, or you can be connected, but not both!" We train boys and men to be dominant and to achieve, and we train girls and women to be gentle and to nurture. Gender role conditioning is all about the subtle and not-so-subtle ways you have been told that your biological sex dictates the menu of choices available to you—the jobs that are appropriate for you, the clothes you can wear, the chores for which you are responsible, and even the shows you can watch! A heterosexual male student of mine shared that he hid his lifelong love of the High School Musical movies for fear of being perceived as not "man enough." This example is benign for sure, but it highlights how sneaky and pervasive these messages are.

Gender role conditioning is alive and well in family life, shaping the stories we are given about the roles we "should" play at home. A home is a small ecosystem, and tasks need to be divided up and assigned in predictable and coordinated ways. If you share a home with someone, think of how annoying it would be to negotiate daily who was going to unload the dishwasher. Homes need divisions of labor. While the traditional male-breadwinner-female-homemaker division of labor has been disrupted in recent years, for sure, that model looms large in our collective awareness. But a model based solely on gender is too rigid, omitting contextual factors like personality, interest, training, and stage of life. If men are "supposed to be" breadwinners and women are "supposed to be" homemakers, then:

- What happens for LGBTQ+ couples?

- What happens when she out-earns him?

- What happens when both partners must work to keep a roof overhead?

- What happens when she is more interested in breadwinning and he is more interested in caregiving?

It is also *hierarchical*. Breadwinning is a higher status role than homemaking, yet the roles are completely interdependent. You cannot eat a paycheck! Income must be converted into goods and services that keep people happy and healthy like groceries, new shoes, and doctors' appointments. The dichotomy between achievement and caregiving tells us a lot about both the nature of gender role conditioning and the nature of work! I wish that we as a culture were "so over this," but my female students frequently describe feeling like they need to decide if they are a career type of woman or a mother type of woman.

While most of today's couples have left behind this rigid paradigm, by design or by necessity, this cultural story casts a long shadow. Men are still sometimes praised for "helping out" with the housework or kids, a compliment that presumes that his caregiving is bonus, demonstrating his willingness to go above and beyond expectations! While we're at it, let's be done saying that the nonprimary caregiver is "babysitting" when they hold down the fort in the absence of the primary caregiver. Lots of women feel crushed by the unpaid and invisible pragmatic and emotional work necessary to manage a household, often in spite of working outside the home as much as their partner. In fact, the demographic most likely to report dissatisfaction with the division of labor at home are women who are married to men.[30]

Although LGBTQ+ couples generally have more equitable divisions of labor than their mixed-gender counterparts, research has found that money matters. The lower-earning partner tends to take charge of cooking and cleaning, and the higher-earning partner tends to handle the budget. And, for both same-sex and mixed-sex couples, those who talk openly about their division of labor are more satisfied than couples who want to talk about it but don't.[31] Domestic life is ripe for resentment, and resentment erodes eroticism. Talking together about roles and routines can help partners feel more aware and appreciative of each other's efforts. Feeling seen and valued is foreplay for sure!

Many of the heterosexual couples in my therapy practice look like Zach and Sarah. Zach and Sarah are in their thirties with two young kids. Sarah left the paid workforce when their first child was born, a decision they made together. Zach has a job, but he isn't earning enough to cover their expenses. They came to therapy because they feel disconnected and discouraged. As I get to know them, the power of our culture's gender story looms large in the room. Her parents seem never to miss an opportunity to slip in comments that convey their opinion that Zach is coming up short in his "duties" as a husband and father.

It's clear that the weight of the situation is taking a toll on Zach, who is irritable and withdrawn. One part of Sarah feels totally at peace with the fact that she will need to seek outside employment, and another part of her feels angry and sad about needing to let go of the picture she had in her head about being home full time during this stage of their family's life. In our sessions, we unpack the heavy yet invisible burden of the gendered story about breadwinning and care-giving. We work on viewing their division of labor in chapters. As Sarah steps into a new job, we work to help Zach feel confident and competent at being the point person in their home. They are "doing" gender very differently than their parents and their grandparents, but our work helps them feel proud of their ability to adapt and flow with their changing demands.

The more they feel like a "we," the less simmering resentment fills the space between them...and the easier it is to make space for sexual connection. The challenge for all busy couples is to figure out how to "de-role" as parents and workers because otherwise, sex feels like another chore or way of taking care of someone else. Zack and Sarah talk with each other about what helps each of them remember that they deserve the pleasure and play that sex offers.

Embodying Agency and Communion

For the last sixty years, researchers have been studying agency and communion as the two "basic modalities of human existence."[32] Agency is about getting stuff done—striving, accomplishing, and leading. Communion is about being connected—nurturing, tending, and caring. These are two ways of "showing up" in the world. One of my mentors, Dan McAdams, writes that agency is associated with "strength, power, expansion, mastery, control, dominance, autonomy, separation, and independence" and communion is associated with "love, friendship, intimacy, sharing, belonging, affiliation, merger, union, nurturance, and so on."[33] The following table outlines the distinction:

Agency	Communion
Self-Mastery	*Love/Friendship*
Status/Victory	*Dialogue*
Achievement/Responsibility	*Caring/Help*
Empowerment	*Unity/Togetherness*

Even though these are simply descriptors of two ways of engaging with the world, under patriarchy, we have long associated agency with being male and communion with being female. However, to live as wholehearted human beings, we must be able to experience ourselves as *both* agentic *and* communal. *We need experiences that make us feel powerful, and we need experiences that make us feel connected!* We are at our best when we can meet both our agentic/masculine needs and our communal/feminine needs. And, as we saw with Zach and Sarah, intimate relationships that can flex and flow enable both partners to express both aspects of their humanity.

Couples who are LGBTQ+ have often done intentional work to deconstruct gendered stories and move into a place of greater wholeness, but heterosexual couples are at somewhat greater risk of replicating in their relationship a problematic split between agency and communion. I spend a lot of time in therapy helping couples address the painful consequences of this split—encouraging men not to label their tears as "weakness" and encouraging women to ask for what they need instead of accommodating everyone around them and simmering with resentment.

If you feel like it is solely your responsibility to maintain relational connection, you will likely experience sex as a service you provide to another person, a way that you take care of them. While Your Sexy likely appreciates the intimacy of communion, Your Sexy also needs access to agency in order to pursue that which feels good and pleasurable.

Think about yourself on a typical day. I guarantee that you could "code" moments of your day during which you are embodying and expressing your *agentic* needs and moments of your day during which you are embodying and expressing your *communal* needs. Here are some examples from my day:

5:45 a.m.: I have chalk on my hands as I work on my clean and jerk at my Crossfit gym.	Agency
11:08 a.m.: I have tears in my eyes as I help a couple work on repairing their marriage.	Communion
1:20 p.m.: I am using a diagram to direct my supervisee on how to work with his client.	Agency
8:07 p.m.: I am tidying up my home and getting ready to play Yahtzee with my kids.	Communion

Reflect on your day and create a table like the one above, identifying the moments of your day when you embodied and expressed communal energy and the moments of the day when you embodied and expressed agentic energy.

- Do you tend to spend more time embodying communal energy or agentic energy?

- Do you make judgments about yourself when you're embodying communal energy? Agentic energy? If so, why might that be? Think about the impact of gendered messages you have internalized.

- At which points of the day do you feel most connected to Your Sexy—at more agentic times or more communal times?

Research indicates that we are healthiest when we can flow between these so-called masculine and feminine ways of being in the world because we need *both* agency *and* communion to live as whole-hearted humans.[34] In fact, one of the most prominent approaches to couples therapy, emotion-focused couples therapy (EFT-C) by Les Greenberg and Rhonda Goldman, is built upon the understanding that couples are at their healthiest (regardless of whether they are mixed-sex or same-sex) when the climate of the couple relationship allows both partners to meet *both* their needs for agency *and* their needs for communion.[35]

A recent meta-analytic review demonstrated that men who ascribe to "sexist beliefs" have poorer mental health.[36] This makes total sense. Sexism blocks our ability to flow between agency and communion. It hurts us as individuals, and it wreaks havoc on intimate relationships. Terry Real explains it this way: "Traditional masculine habits not only hurt men's physical and psychological health, but also produce the least happy marriages. Study after study has shown that egalitarian marriages—which often involve dual careers and always encompass shared housework and decision making—unequivocally lead to higher rates of marital satisfaction for both sexes than do 'traditional' marriages, based on hierarchy and a strict division of roles."[37] For everyone's sake, it's time to stop associating agency with men and communion with women, and we need to stop worshipping agency and holding communion in contempt.

Great Sex Is the Flow of Agency and Communion

Sexual interactions are more powerfully shaped by our gender role conditioning than any other interactions.[38] This means that in the realm of intimate relationships, we feel especially pressured to conform to the gendered code of conduct we've internalized from our culture. When someone living in a male body and someone living in a female body have sex, it's so easy for that ancient, rigid sexual script to lead the way. One of my clients, Yasmine, shared with me, "Masculine energy seems to be synonymous with being rough and in control. Sex seems to be built on this, that men will lead and take control, while women accept and give. It leaves no room for women to explore their own needs. My partner now constantly asks me what I want, and the role reversal or shift of expectation is daunting. It challenges everything I've been taught about how women are conditioned to engage in sex."

Yasmine is wrestling with deeply entrenched sexual constructs, which is understandable because these messages are reinforced everywhere, including in porn. Men take the lead, often roughly and forcefully. Women are passive, and, according to much of what we see in porn, 100 percent ecstatic about their passivity.[39] Yasmine's story also highlights that when a woman is partnered with someone who really values her experience of pleasure, it can feel *both* affirming *and* daunting. To advocate for your pleasure, you need to know what feels good to you, and you need to be able ask for it! We will explore those challenges in the coming chapters, but in the meantime, I want to highlight something else.

If your partner is male, he likely brings into a sexual experience his conditioning that his worth and manliness rest on (A) his ability to "perform" by keeping an erection and (B) your orgasm. In the case of B, his attempt to *give* might end up feeling to you like another version of a *take*. Peel back the layers of the overtly generous question, "How can I make you come?" and you may find that what he's really saying is, "I need you to come to regulate my sense of self-worth because I was raised in a culture that taught me to fix stuff, and right now your arousal is a problem I need to solve!" Now, rather than a playful space of pleasure, escape, and connection, you are both getting effed by the patriarchy! He feels pressured to give you an orgasm so he feels man enough, and you feel pressured to have an orgasm so he doesn't feel badly about himself. It's no wonder that research has found that most women fake their orgasms at least some of the time. Please believe that we're gonna come back to that topic later because it's a doozy!

Let's stay focused on this active-passive split and look at the good stuff that can happen when we free ourselves from it. A couple of years ago, I attended a clinical training led by sex therapist Tammy Nelson, and part of the workshop was a panel discussion with members of the local *kink community.* Kink is broadly defined as sexual practices that exist beyond what has been defined as conventional or "vanilla," including various fetishes and BDSM (a catch-all phrase that encompasses bondage discipline, dominance, submission and sadism, and masochism). I was struck by how much the "vanilla" world can learn from those whose sexualities have been maligned and relegated to the margins of "polite" society. The heterosexual sexual script is chock-full of assumptions about who does what to whom in bed, so those who step away from that narrow and rigid script are gifted the opportunity to negotiate and create whatever the heck they want. The sexual experience becomes a blank canvas. *A central feature of the kink community is consciously exploring what is possible at the intersection of sex and power.*

Power gets a bad rap because it is so frequently abused, but power is simply the ability to act on your environment. Power is agency. In sex that reflexively follows a traditional heterosexual script, he has all of it, and she has none of it. Power is enacted implicitly, silently, automatically, and unconsciously. The kink community is curious about "dancing with" power in an explicit and conscious way as a means of enhancing pleasure and play through something called *power exchange*. Power exchange may refer to a relationship in which one person is the "dominant" and the other is the "submissive," or it may refer to a sexual experience in which there is agreement about who is in charge. Partners decide together who will lead and who will follow, as there is much pleasure to be experienced in each of these roles.

You may never dip a toe into the waters of kink, or you may already be a full-fledged kinky swimmer. Either way, Your Sexy will surely appreciate the opportunity to bust up the tired story that the only role available to women is one of passivity, submission, silence, and compliance. Playing with creative possibilities for leading and following in the bedroom will open you to new experiences of Your Sexy. All exploration of power must rest upon a foundation of enthusiastic and juicy consent, which is what we'll tackle next.

The Only Yes Is Yes

As a gender studies major at the University of Michigan in the 1990s, I participated in many Take Back the Night rallies, gathering with women and allies to end sexual violence. Our signs and our rally cries were all about, "No means no." Looking back, it is tragic that a definition of consent would start and finish with the notion that if somebody says no, you need to stop. Stopping if someone says no is an incredibly low bar, one that makes zero space for discussions about pleasure, mutual enthusiasm, and cocreating a fun and respect-filled experience. No means no is a fine place to start, but we need so much more. Let's start with some more information about consent, taken from RAINN's website (Rape, Abuse, and Incest National Network).[40]

What Is Consent?

Consent is an agreement between participants to engage in sexual activity. There are many ways to give consent, and some of those are discussed below. Consent doesn't have to be verbal, but verbally agreeing to different sexual activities can help both you and your partner respect each other's boundaries.

How Does Consent Work in Real Life?

When you're engaging in sexual activity, *consent is about communication*. And it should happen every time. Giving consent for one activity, one time, does not mean giving consent for increased or recurring sexual contact. For example, agreeing to kiss someone doesn't give that person permission to remove your clothes. Having sex with someone in the past doesn't give that person permission to have sex with you again in the future.

You Can Change Your Mind at Any Time

You can withdraw consent at any point if you feel uncomfortable. It's important to clearly communicate to your partner that you are no longer comfortable with this activity and wish to stop. The best way to ensure both parties are comfortable with any sexual activity is to talk about it.

Positive consent can look like this:

- Communicating when you change the type or degree of sexual activity with phrases like, "Is this okay?"

- Explicitly agreeing to certain activities, either by saying "yes," or another affirmative statement, like "I'm open to trying"

- Using physical cues to let the other person know you're comfortable taking things to the next level

It does *not* look like this:

- Refusing to acknowledge "no"

- Assuming that wearing certain clothes, flirting, or kissing is an invitation for anything more

- Someone being under the legal age of consent, as defined by the state

- Someone being incapacitated because of drugs or alcohol

- Pressuring someone into sexual activity by using fear or intimidation

- Assuming you have permission to engage in a sexual act because you've done it in the past

The RAINN information states this, but it bears repeating—if you're saying yes because you feel you have to in order to avoid a negative outcome, that's coercion, and it's not okay. Your "no" is a complete sentence, and a partner who presses once you've declined is not operating from a place of mutuality, care, or respect. Giving a guilt trip ("But you've been teasing me all night"), negotiating ("How about just a blow job?"), or behaving in a threatening or manipulative manner ("I'm going to tell my friends you did, so you may as well") are all examples of coercion.

Consent is about empathically guided feedback loops. Partner A makes an invitation, "Can I kiss you?" Partner B checks in with themselves—does this invitation feel like a big ole yes or a big ole no? If it's a big ole yes, partner B says, "I would *love* that!" That's how enthusiastically consensual sexual experiences go. They are a series of give-and-takes and questions and answers, putting a possibility into the space between you and your partner and seeing if your partner is game for it. Passion *and* empathy. Far from mutually exclusive, excitement and care can and should readily occupy the same space at the same time.

We can't talk about sex without talking about gender role conditioning. Expectations of who can ask for what from whom are so rigid when it comes to sex. These old stories are intimacy-limiting, and they dull creativity and possibility. When we commit to viewing ourselves and our partners as whole beings, we free ourselves up to create healthier and more self-aware sexual experiences.

�֎

Talking about gender dynamics sometimes puts people on the defensive. Although these problems are far too big for blame, words like "feminism" and "patriarchy" hold the power to shut people down. Conversations about the impact of gender-role conditioning need to happen in a space far beyond blame and shame so we can entertain new possibilities for how each of us inhabits agency and communion. That's what Your Sexy is craving! While Your Sexy is gendered, that gendered nature is rich and refusing of simplification, and you are better positioned to advocate for what you need sexually when you give yourself permission to flow between the energies of agency and communion, giving and receiving, expressing and connecting.

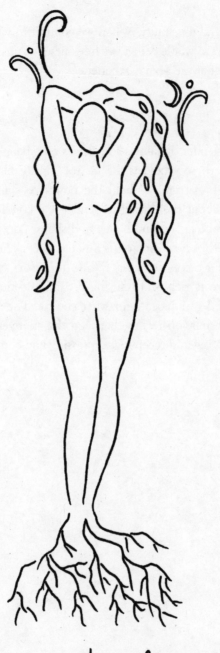

developmental

Your Sexy Is a Glorious and Unfolding Story

Being able to exercise your own choice can bring about greater opportunity. I think it's just as important what you say no to as what you say yes to.

—Sandra Oh, *Vanity Fair* interview

Meet Maeve, a college-aged woman who has one of my favorite stories ever about a turning-point moment that forever changed her relationship with Her Sexy:

I had had several casual sexual experiences with guys on campus. I had never even considered my pleasure. I felt okay stopping a guy if I felt like he wanted to do more than I wanted to do, but I hadn't really ever considered what I wanted pleasure-wise. Until I started hooking up with Nick. The first time we were making out, he said, "Do you want me to take your shirt off?" I did what I always had done. I shrugged my shoulders and said, "If you want to." He stopped and looked at me and said, "There are too many guys who just keep going as long as a girl isn't saying no. That's not me. Whatever we do, we're gonna do because you want to do it." I had no framework for this. It felt weird but good. Since that experience, I am so different in the bedroom. I communicate what I want and what I don't want, and if a guy isn't interested in hearing that, I feel really comfortable shutting the whole thing down. The relationship with Nick didn't work out, but I'm so grateful for what I learned from being with him!

Maeve felt embarrassed that she had gotten this far without knowing that she could and should consider what she wants from her sexual experiences. But, like all of us, she is a product of her environment. Pleasure was not talked about in her school's sex ed program. Her father died when she was fourteen, so during her teen years, she and her mother focused exclusively on keeping their heads above water emotionally and financially. Maeve didn't date, and she and her mom really didn't talk about sex. She had watched some porn, talked with her friends about sex, and internalized a bunch of societal messages. She had dutifully downloaded the obligatory heterosexual script of male pursuer and female gatekeeper as the only template for sex.

I don't know the backstory on Nick, but I know that our world needs more men like him! He knows that the absence of a "no" is an unacceptably low bar when it comes to consent. He also knows that wonderful sexual experiences happen when two people are connected to what they want and are therefore able to *cocreate* a big, juicy "hell yes!" In her hookup with Nick, Maeve learned that her desire can and should be an integral factor in her sexual experiences.

Maeve's experience with Nick reminds us that you get to be a life-long learner, integrating experiences, knowledge, and aha moments into the story of Your Sexy. But let's be clear: You do *not* need to wait around for a Nick to show up in your life, granting you permission to connect with your sexual desire. *You are your own Nick.* And you deserve only those sexual partners who understand that great sex is co-constructed every step of the way.

Your Sexy Is Alive

Development is the second place we need to visit on our Map of Sexual Self-Awareness. Your sexuality is a glorious and unfolding story, and you are the author. Who you are sexually at nineteen years old is different from who you are sexually at thirty-nine years old, and it sure as heck is different from who you are sexually at seventy-nine years old. The thread that runs through these chapters is YOU.

When I think about how this deep truth feels in my own life, I get that dizzy-woozy-whoa feeling. Though my husband has been my intimate partner for many years, there exist within our marriage *three sexualities*—his, mine, and ours. Each of these sexualities is dynamic and unfolding. The sexual experiences we had early in our relationship (fueled by early attraction...and fear of unplanned pregnancy) are different from the sexual experiences we have now (fueled by affection and attachment) and are different from the sexual experiences we will (hopefully!) have years from now.

Thinking about Your Sexy as an unfolding story is a massive invitation to self-compassion. You are doing the best you can. You can only know what you know right now. Lean into a deep and gentle trust that you *have been* writing, you *are* writing, and you *will keep* writing the story of Your Sexy. That trust gives you the latitude you need to wonder, explore, and figure out how to evaluate your experiences. And, from a place of greater awareness, shed patterns that don't work for you so that you can make choices that feel affirming and aligned.

We need to start by talking about desire—the science of sexual desire, what happens when partners have different ways of experiencing sexual desire, and how to understand your motivations for having sex (either casual sex or relationship sex). My hope for you is twofold: that you will view your relationship to desire as one that will continue to unfold over time and that you will own what Your Sexy needs in order to joyfully enter a sexual space with a partner.

Know Your Why: The Art and Science of Sexual Desire

In a society that barely provides us with a basic understanding of what sex is, most of us are ill-equipped to consider *why* we have it. The why of sex changes across a sexual experience, across the course of a relationship, and across a lifespan. The why of sex is complicated. The why of sex gets us to an important topic: sexual desire. Sexual desire is defined as a motivational state, and it is the most universally experienced sexual response.[41] Sexual desire is an interest in or an openness to entering a sexual space. Esther Perel says that to desire is "to own the wanting." The more you can make peace with the fact that sexual desire is a state (temporary and dynamic), not a trait (permanent and static), the more you can be Your Sexy's best advocate and ally. You know by now that when it comes to sex, there are no easy answers, so understanding how desire operates for you is going to take some unpacking.

Lucky for us, we have researchers and clinicians who have been studying this stuff for years, and their research can help us out. The earliest teams of sex researchers in the United States developed the Masters-Johnson-Kaplan Model of Sexual Response (shown in the image below).[42] For many years, this model was the foundation for all the teaching about human sexuality, the diagnosing of sexual dysfunctions, and the planning of treatment. It charted a universal and linear series of phases of sexual response: desire, arousal, plateau, orgasm, and resolution.

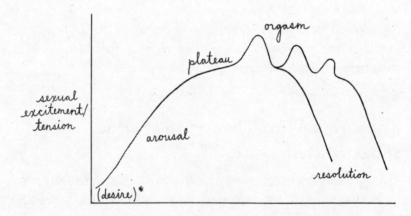

The Masters-Johnson-Kaplan Model of Sexual Response

After the publication of this chart, something funky started to happen. An awful lot of women were diagnosed with sexual problems, specifically sexual desire problems. One study found that 43 percent of American women met the criteria for a sexual dysfunction.[43]

Before this story totally bums you out, we need to cue the feisty heroines who wear lab coats instead of capes! This next generation of sex researchers began to dig into this finding that lots of otherwise sexually functioning and relationally satisfied women were reporting low or absent desire. Rather than deeming vast swaths of the female population to be "pathological," researchers began to question the model. Rosemary Basson proposed an alternative model that better describes the sexual response of many women and some men and that highlights the diverse routes we may take into a sexual space.[44] Take a look at her model below.

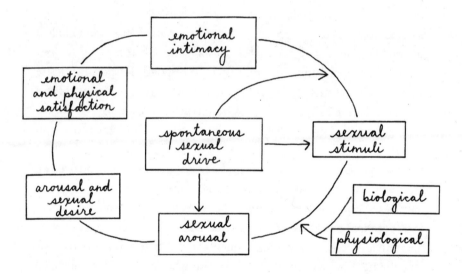

Basson's Model of Sexual Motivation

Historically, "the presence of sexual thoughts, fantasies, and an innate urge to experience sexual tension and release, alone or with a partner, have been considered the markers for desire."[45] But when women are asked what motivates them to agree to or initiate a sexual experience with their partner, their lists are extensive, varied, and intimacy-based. Basson says these lists include, "wanting to be emotionally close, to show love and affection, to share physical pleasure for the sake of sharing, to increase a sense of attractiveness and attraction, to increase a sense of commitment and bonding, but only sometimes to satisfy a truly 'sexual' need."[46]

Researchers began considering two types of sexual desire: "spontaneous desire" and "responsive desire." Spontaneous desire comes in the form of sexual thoughts and urges or physiological cues. Spontaneous desire sounds like this, *Damn, sex would feel really good right now!* Responsive desire is context-specific and sounds more like this: You and your partner are watching a show on the couch. She leans over and starts to kiss your neck. Your first thoughts are, *It's so late, I have a little headache, and I haven't brushed my teeth.* But then your next thoughts are, *That does feel kind of good, I love feeling close to her, and I know I'll feel glad that we've done it.* So, you respond to your partner's advances and trust your body to respond. Responsive desire is about being motivated *less* by an internal sensation of horniness and *more* by relational experiences, environmental cues, and/or the knowledge that your desire tends to catch up with you if and when you lean into it.

By recognizing that desire can be spontaneous or responsive, we are acknowledging that people have varied motivations for wanting to have sex. Spontaneous desire may be a reality for only some women, and perhaps more likely in the context of a new relationship. Spontaneous desire may be infrequent or absent in a large portion of sexually healthy women, especially those who are in well-established intimate relationships. Arousal may precede desire, meaning that she may enter a sexual space with her partner feeling sexually neutral but emotionally willing. Then, as she seeks and receives sexual stimuli, she moves from neutrality to sexual arousal. Think about responsive desire as a feedback loop: the better it feels (physically and emotionally) for her to be in this sexual space with her partner, the more she wants to continue the experience, and the more she continues, the more aroused she feels.

How fitting that a linear model may better approximate male sexual desire and a curvy model may better approximate female sexual desire! When I show this diagram to audiences, the men (at least the ones who have sex with women) invariably look at each other and let out a groan because at first glance it looks so darned complicated. "Stop that!" I snap at the groaners. "I'm about to give you some vital information that has the power to improve your sex life!" It's also not altogether clear to me whether men truly feel overwhelmed by the diagram or whether they feel a need to play out the cultural trope that men are always ready for sex and women need coaxing and convincing. In fact, new research indicates that male sexual desire may be similarly responsive to relational and contextual cues.[47] The bottom line is that until we transform cultural messages about who is allowed to ask for and enjoy sex, our constructions of sexual desire are approximations.

Let's look more closely at Basson's model. This diagram shows that a sexual experience may be fueled by spontaneous desire ("I want sex!"), indicated by the center circle. But you can see that there's another pathway. On this path, sex is sparked relationally. *Emotional intimacy, emotional satisfaction, and physical satisfaction* can create sexual motivation. Feeling close and safe creates sexual openness. *Receptivity to sexual stimuli* can also create the possibility for arousal. In other words, willingness is step one, and arousal fuels desire. *The big takeaway is that sexual desire is more complicated than sex therapists once thought, and knowledge is power.* Before we talk about how you can use this information to support Your Sexy, take the quiz below to see whether you tend to have spontaneous desire, responsive desire, both, or something else!

This quiz is used with permission from Nowosielski, Wrobel, and Kowalczyk.[48]

The following four statements attempt to describe women's sexual response. Please read them and then check which, if any, you feel best describes your own sexual experiences with your current or most recent partner (one answer only).

Model 1. Before sexual activity with my partner, I feel excited (I am turned on). Then, I become more excited, and usually, I reach orgasm(s). Sometimes, I start sexual activity with my partner when I feel the desire for sex or I am "in the mood." During our sexual activities, I become aroused, and as the sensation is building, I may have orgasm(s).

Model 2. I agree to have sex with my partner for reasons other than sexual desire (for example, I want to be closer to my partner or to experience intimacy with him [sic]). Usually, before we start, I do not feel "in the mood" to have sex. However, when we start caressing and touching each other, I become excited (aroused). The feeling of desire for sex appears in different moments. During or at the end of our sexual activity, I feel satisfied, and when it gets more intense, I feel more desire and want to continue. When the sexual sensations are building, I may have an orgasm or orgasms.

Model 3. I experience model 1 and model 2 in similar proportions during my sexual activities.

Model 4. My sexual response is different from the above models.

If model 1 sounds like you, you primarily experience spontaneous desire. If you answered model 2, you primarily experience responsive desire. If you answered model 3, you experience both spontaneous and responsive desire, like Basson's Model of Sexual Motivation. If you answered model 4, your sexual response doesn't fit neatly into any of these categories.

In a sample of heterosexual, partnered women, researchers found that 28.7 percent of the survey's participants tended to experience spontaneous desire; 19.5 percent of participants tended to experience responsive desire; 40.8 percent of participants experienced some combination of spontaneous and responsive desire; and 10.9 percent of participants experienced desire that lay outside of these categories. These data show us that it is most common for women to experience a combination of sexual and nonsexual reasons for entering a sexual space with their partners. *Knowing that there are multiple pathways into a sexual experience is so permission-giving.* It's a massive invitation to drop shame-loaded stories and to instead work with what you've got!

When someone who experiences spontaneous desire is partnered with someone who experiences responsive desire, it's so easy to get caught up in stories that make both partners feel worse. Morgan and Karen have been together for five years. Morgan tends to experience spontaneous desire, and Karen mostly experiences responsive desire. In the early days of the relationship, both partners initiated sex, but Morgan has begun to feel frustrated about always being the initiator. Most of the time, Morgan accepts that this is just how the relationship functions, but at times Morgan slips into a shame-loaded story that Karen no longer finds Morgan attractive. Karen feels confused and upset about what's happening to her. She loves Morgan so much, and when they have sex, she really enjoys the experience, physically and emotionally. Most of the time, she accepts this situation, but at times, she finds herself slipping into a shame-loaded story that something must be wrong with her. It's easy to see how these stories can take on a life of their own—I'm broken, my partner is broken, and/or our relationship is doomed.

These stories are toxic, widening the space between partners and creating silence that prevents much-needed collaboration. Lucky for Morgan and Karen, they began to learn about the nature of sexual desire. This knowledge empowered them to work together to cultivate the conditions of desire within each of them and between the two of them. They have found it intimacy-producing to stand shoulder to shoulder and talk together about their sexual relationship. They will come back again and again to this shared language as they evolve over time, individually and as a couple. Beyond the relief and compassion that come from simply knowing that there are multiple pathways into sex, they found it empowering to get specific about their unique sexual cues. It's time for you to get specific too!

Vroom Vroom: Your Sexy Is Like a Car

Your Sexy is like a car in that you have an engine (sexual arousal) that is controlled by a gas pedal and a brake.[49] Sexual researchers call this the "dual control model" (DCM).[50] Your sexual response has to do with the balance of excitatory (good-yummy-more) and inhibitory (bad-yucky-stop) processes happening in your brain. Your sexual response in any given sexual experience depends on the degree to which you are coding the situation as a good-yummy-more situation versus as a bad-yucky-stop situation. According to the DCM:

- There's lots of variability in how us human beings "do" sexual excitation and sexual inhibition.

- In situations where sexual activity could be dangerous, it is adaptive or healthy to experience sexual inhibition.

- How you "do" sexual excitation and sexual inhibition is shaped by your personality, your past experiences, and your context.[51]

Understanding where you fall on the spectrum of both sexual inhibition and sexual excitation expands your sexual self-awareness. Look at the table below (taken from the incredible work of Emily Nagoski) and see if you can figure out how you would rate both your sexual excitation system (SES) and your sexual inhibition system (SIS).

Remember that there is no good or bad and there is no right or wrong. This is just information. Resist the urge to label your gas and brake as anything other than exactly as they are. Gathering this information is step 1, and step 2 is figuring out what (if anything) you want to do about it. Remember, too, that your gas and brake are dynamic. Becoming more sexually self-aware and living in greater alignment with Your Sexy may change your gas and brake.

If you conclude that you have a sensitive brake and a rather reluctant accelerator, your first order of business is to accept this piece of information exactly as it is. As brilliant spiritual teacher, Byron Katie, says, "When I argue with reality, I lose. But only 100 percent of the time."[52] Resist the urge to craft a shame-loaded story about what you think this says about you as a woman! Acceptance is the best place from which to act because it allows you to sit with loving possibilities. You might do nothing at all. You might opt to use your growing sexual self-awareness to create some you-specific practices that stoke Your Sexy.

The same principle of radical self-acceptance holds if what you've learned is that you have a sensitive accelerator and a hard-to-engage brake. All you need to do is ask yourself, "How can I use this information in the service of My Sexy?" Perhaps there's nothing to do. Just keep on keeping on! Or maybe you check in with yourself about the degree to which you may use sex to regulate your anxiety. While sex can surely be an amazing stress-reliever, any coping strategy (eating, drinking, shopping, exercising) can be overused. Would you benefit from adding other tools to your stress-management toolbox?

Sexual Excitation System (SES)

Low SES You have a harder-to-press gas pedal.	You don't readily code the sexually relevant "stuff" that is around you. You may need to be more intentional to get in the mood. You may need some more intensity (from a vibrator or from erotic materials for example) in order to get aroused.
Medium SES You have a moderately hard-to-press gas pedal.	Your sensitivity to sexual stimuli depends on the context. Your Sexy will benefit from cultivating erotic contexts that cue you that sex is a great option.
High SES You have an easy-to-press gas pedal.	You readily tune in to sexual cues, even ones like smells and tastes, and a wide range of contexts can awaken Your Sexy.

Sexual Inhibition System (SIS)

Low SIS You don't have much of a brake.	You don't worry much about your sexual functioning. Body image concerns don't get in your way. You're not sexually shy. You may struggle to rein yourself in and think through potential consequences of your choices.
Medium SIS You have a moderate brake.	You are sensitive to context. Stress may make you put on the brakes. Safety and familiarity with a partner may keep you from hitting your brakes.
High SIS You have an easy-to-press brake.	You tend to be really in touch with all the reasons not to be aroused. You need a lot of trust and relaxation. You may get easily distracted during sex. You may be somewhat more at risk of experiencing something like low sexual desire.

Getting in the Zone

In addition to understanding the fact that Your Sexy runs on this DCM, it's helpful to get specific about what helps you transition from the ordinary world to the erotic world so you can be Your Sexy's best advocate. A team of researchers interviewed women, ages eighteen to twenty-nine, about the nature of their sexual desire and found that these are major the factors that either inhibited or elicited their sexual desire:

- Their energy level

- Feeling sexy

- Physical attraction to their partner

- Their partner's attentiveness

- Intimate communication

- Life transitions

- The possibility of pregnancy[53]

You can see from this list that sexual desire is impacted by a variety of factors: how I feel, how I feel about me, how I feel about you, how I feel about us, and how I feel about life.

Now that you understand the DCM of sexual desire, it's time to get specific about your accelerators and your brakes. These exercises are based on Emily Nagoski's work.

Sexy Contexts

Sit quietly, close your eyes, and settle in. Think about a really positive sexual experience. This could be a sexual experience that you've actually had, or it could be one that you would be interested in having. Once you've spent some time imagining this scene, write about what made it so positive, making sure you include these aspects:

- How you were feeling mentally and physically

- The characteristics of your partner

- The characteristics of the relationship

- The setting (Where were you? What was happening before?)

- The storyline (Who was doing what to whom?)

Not-So-Sexy Contexts

Once again, sit quietly, close your eyes, and settle in. Think about a disappointing or less-than-great sexual experience. When you are ready, write about what made it not-so-good, making sure you include these aspects:

- How you were feeling mentally and physically

- The characteristics of your partner

- The characteristics of the relationship

- The setting (Where were you? What was happening before?)

- The storyline (Who was doing what to whom?)

Write about both of these exercises. What do you notice? What surprised you? What are your takeaways?

Your Sexy, My Sexy, Our Sexy

If you are in an intimate relationship, learn more about your partner's gas pedal and brake. If there's a great deal of similarity between you and your partner in terms of your sexy contexts, it might be relatively simple for you to work together to figure out practices that keep you sexually connected. If there are differences between the two of you, proceed with care. The crucial task of all intimate relationships is to navigate differences with empathy and grace. Simple. But not easy. When we are face-to-face with a difference (partner A: "When I am stressed out, sex is a great stress-reliever," versus partner B: "When I am stressed out, I can't even think about having sex"), our knee-jerk reaction is to view our way as the good/better/normal way and our partner's way the bad/worse/weird way.

The moment we attach ourselves to a judgmental story is the moment we begin to head down a path toward distress and distance. Instead, we need to view the difference between us as fascinating…or at least perplexing and worthy of deeper exploration. When you meet the difference with a sense of curiosity, you can work together on what this means for your sexual relationship. I adore this adage: "The first thing you should know about me is that I am not you. A lot more will make sense after that." Treat these differences as intriguing, not threatening, and use the Golden Equation of Love to help you innovate together, figuring out how to be fellow travelers on an erotic journey. We will talk more about this in chapter 9.

From Fear to Love: Sexual Motivation

Practicing sexual self-awareness involves looking at what motives you to have sex. Sometimes, the answer is simple, "It's sex, and I want it!" Sometimes the answer is a bit more complicated. Sexual motivators can be broken down into two categories: "approach motivations" and "avoidance motivations." When you look at these, they will remind you of the love versus fear distinction from chapter 2.

Approach motivations are about seeking what you want: closeness, affection, pleasure, escape, orgasm, stress relief, or help falling asleep. Approach motivations are fueled by the energy of love.

Avoidance motivations are about preventing what you don't want: abandonment, conflict, embarrassment, or guilt if you don't have sex. Avoidance motivations are fueled by the energy of fear.

Some motivators can readily be classified as approach or avoidance, but how would you classify the following common motivator? *"I'm going to have sex with my partner because I know they want to."* Is this an approach motivation because it's about having sex to enhance connection? Or is this an avoidance motivation because it's about having sex to avoid the guilt you might feel if you don't? As with most everything related to love and sex, there's no easy answer, and context clarifies. Motivation that is in response to your partner's desire for sex is called "sexual communal strength."[54] Nurturing intimacy and connection requires partners to extend themselves in all kinds of ways—sexual and otherwise. In a happy relationship, sex can be a fun gift to give your eager partner, but if and when you extend yourself in order to make your partner happy, keep these four ingredients in the mix:

1. **Pride.** If you are showing up for sex with your partner even though you feel tired, you are making a deposit into the relationship bank account, and you deserve to feel proud of yourself for doing so. Without pride, resentment will take root, and we know that nothing dulls Your Sexy faster than feeling like a martyr!

2. **Reciprocity.** It's much easier to motivate yourself using sexual communal strength when you are in touch with all the ways that your partner "shows up" for you too. To what degree are you asking for what you need in the relationship? To what degree does your partner honor your needs versus dismiss or judge them?

3. **Flexibility.** Sometimes sexual communal strength motivates a reluctant partner to kick Their Sexy into gear. But this is a

two-way street. Sometimes a higher-desire partner takes sex off the table for their partner's sake. Relationships are happier and healthier when that happens some of the time as well.[55]

4. **Self-advocacy.** Consider what you need to make the experience as amazing as possible for you. Keep some "I" in "we." A little bit of selfishness is a very good thing. With self-advocacy, what had been a story of "I'm doing this for you" becomes a win-win.

While sexual communal strength enhances an otherwise happy and healthy relationship, you certainly *never* owe sex to anyone under any circumstances. A partner begging you for sex will trigger your sexual brakes for sure, and sulking is a far cry from seducing.

Also, if your motivators are largely avoidance based, it is a red flag, and you should lovingly and gently address what's going on for you. Perhaps you are early in your journey to take Your Sexy back, and you just need some time and practice tapping into your right to pleasure and sexual expression. But maybe something else is going on. Perhaps your partner is coercive about sex, and you are stuck in an unhealthy cycle of blame and shame that needs to be addressed. The "Additional Resources for Your Sexy" section at the back of this book has some resources to help you find a therapist. A therapist can help you and your partner break out of this toxic pattern…or help you end the relationship.

Or perhaps your struggle with desire warrants a deeper look. Remember how under the old definition of sexual desire disorders, almost half of women met the criteria for a sexual interest or arousal disorder? With this new distinction between spontaneous and responsive desire, we also have a new definition of sexual desire disorder. The disorder is now called sexual interest/arousal disorder (SIAD), and in order to be diagnosed with SIAD, someone needs to be experiencing at least three of the following:

- Absent or reduced interest in sexual activity

- Absent or reduced erotic thoughts or fantasies

- No or reduced initiation of sexual activity, and typically unreceptive to a partner's attempts to initiate

- Absent or reduced sexual pleasure during most or all sexual encounters

- Absent or reduced sexual interest or arousal in response to internal or external sexual cues

- Absent/reduced physical sexual sensations.

In addition to the above, the person also needs to be experiencing the following two symptoms between most or all of the time (75 to 100 percent of the time): absent or reduced sexual excitement and absent or reduced pleasant genital sensations. The bad news is that this new diagnosis is still somewhat controversial.[56] The good news is that there is more interest than ever in understanding female sexual desire! If after reading this book you still feel concerned that something more serious is going on for you, connect with a sex therapist.

Hookup Sex Versus Self-Aware Casual Sex

At some points along the way, sex outside of the context of a committed relationship may be an amazing choice for you. A committed relationship may not be a good fit for any number of reasons—you're studying, traveling, grieving, recovering, whatever! Sexual experiences that happen outside of a marriage—both relationship sex and casual sex—are far less stigmatized today than they historically were. With fewer outside-in restrictions about where, when, and with whom you have sex, you need to figure out, from the inside-out, what works for you.

I find it helpful to make the distinction between *hookup sex* and *self-aware casual sex* because it helps us address the key (and often ignored) issue: *motivation*. Hookup sex is something you just sort of fall into. It is characterized by low communication, low empathy, little to no after-care (checking in with each other the next day) and, usually, a ton of alcohol. Rather than being driven by sexual pleasure or sexual exploration, hookup sex tends to be fueled by two separate but related fear-based motivations:

- I "should" do this so that I can be seen as chill, no-drama, or sexually liberated.

- I "should" do this because it might lead to an intimate relationship.

In the first case, the problem is an intimate-justice problem. Cynicism about love or struggles with self-worth fuel a sense that you simply can't ask for more than low-accountability and low-intimacy sexual experiences. The second case is mixed-agenda sex or hidden-agenda sex—an attempted means to an end. Here, hookup sex is filled with an underlying, and often unspoken, wish that sex will lead to the thing that is really yearned for—a relationship.

By contrast, self-aware casual sex is cocreated. It is two people coming together in an intentional way and saying to each other some version of, "I'm not in a good place to commit to an intimate relationship right now. A casual sexual relationship is all I am offering. Let's figure out whether and how we can create a space for mutual pleasure and play." You need to make agreements about boundaries: Are we also sleeping with other people? How are we protecting our sexual health? What kind of after-care does each of us need and want? Self-aware casual sex is founded on mutual exploration and respect for a shared interest in separating pleasure from commitment.

The shift from hookup sex to self-aware casual sex is the shift from resignation ("This is the most I can expect from relationships") to declaration ("Here's what I am available for"). Same act, different underlying narrative. Listening to Your Sexy will help you get clear on sexual boundaries that feel aligned and healthy for you.

Of Boundaries and Catching Feelings

Although college is a bit of an atypical microcosm, the following findings are worth sharing. On any given night on a college campus, two-thirds of the hookups are repeat performances, and nearly half of women and about a third of men hope that the hookup will become a relationship.[57] If your deep truth is that you'd like to be in a committed romantic relationship, hooking up may leave you feeling dissatisfied—still wanting a relationship and now processing some amount of shame and disconnection from Your Sexy. Given that dating and hooking up have become practically synonymous, sorting this out is a challenge! It can feel like low accountability hookups are the good/right/normal/liberated/only way to be sexual.

But hookup sex that is not motivated by your authentic choice and not centered on your sexual needs is problematic, especially for women who have sex with men. Hookup sex is unfortunately a high-risk endeavor, as most unwanted sexual experiences on college campuses occur in the context of a hookup.[58] Further, only 11 percent of women report having an orgasm during a first-time hookup with a male partner compared to 67 percent of women who report having an orgasm during relationship sex with a male partner.[59] While orgasm isn't everything, this data conveys something compelling about intimate justice. Finally, over half (54 percent) of heterosexual women report feeling that their partner respected them less after a hookup (versus only 22 percent of heterosexual men who reported feeling this way).[60]

Researchers Elizabeth Armstrong, Paula England, and Alison Fogarty state that the increase in nonrelationship sex has created a *new sexual double standard*. The old double standard was shaming women far more than their male counterparts for having premarital sex at all—a stigma that has all but disappeared except in religiously conservative communities.[61] The new sexual double standard is judging women more harshly than men for seeking sexual pleasure outside of the context of a committed relationship. As these researchers say, "The new double standard also involves judgments about appropriate levels of sexual enthusiasm or initiative, as men are assumed to have a strong, active drive to seek sex, whereas women are viewed as more sexually passive, responding to men's desire."[62]

This new double standard can keep you from feeling entitled to pleasure for fear of being seen as "controlling" or "slutty." If your partner is a guy, this double standard might keep *him* from feeling a sense of responsibility to accommodate your sexual needs. The more his behavior indicates that your pleasure doesn't matter, the harder it is to ask for what you need. A silencing cycle for sure! Tragically, this fear of being maligned for being proactive leaves some women who have sex with men feeling self-conscious about buying and carrying condoms. This double standard compromises mutuality, creativity, and connection. You deserve to have sex that is grounded in what motivates you and feels good to you, and that starts with listening carefully and lovingly to Your Sexy. Be clear. You can't do it alone. You need and deserve a partner who is similarly committed to being sexually self-aware.

Casual sexual relationships can certainly run their course and end amicably. However, even the most well-articulated casual sexual arrangements can be perfect in theory and messy in execution, ending in heartbreak because one partner ends up wanting more than casual sex. To mitigate this risk, stay attuned to your internal world. If you feel your motivation shift from wanting exploration, pleasure, and sexual growth to wanting a deeper emotional relationship and greater commitment, be courageous and talk with your partner. Drop the story that "catching feelings" means that you failed.

Although even the most clearly stated boundaries can be violated, clearly defined boundaries will help you maximize pleasure and fun while keeping you safe. It's also far easier to track internal shifts in your motivation and desire when you're clear about your boundaries. Consider the following questions: What have your past sexual encounters taught you about your boundaries? Which sexual acts are in or out of bounds? Which areas of the body are in or out of bounds? What forms of sexual protection do you want or need to use? What fantasies are or aren't you willing to explore with this person? What sexual positions do you enjoy, and which are you definitely not trying? What are the other limits you might need in the bedroom, and how do you want to respond if something new or unexpected comes up?

Answer these questions for yourself so that you are clear where your boundaries are. Then take it a step further and think about how you can convey this information to your partner. If you have been raised to be demure and people-pleasing, this courageous conversation might be much easier said than done. You might find it helpful to visualize this conversation before you have it. Imagine what it might be like for you to communicate your answers to the above questions with a partner. Imagine the types of responses you would expect to hear. Imagine how you might respond to hearing a partner's answers to these questions.

A Tale of Two Sexies

Two of my students, who are good friends, Beth and Alana, have had vastly different experiences with sex outside of a relationship, and their stories highlight the need to get clear on the nature of your desire. Beth is in her late twenties and in a long-term relationship now, but she participated in hookup culture throughout college and into her early twenties. Casual hookups often left her feeling ashamed and disconnected from her own body. She always wanted to be desired and to have the companionship of a man, but she felt unable to find this in ways other than participating in hookup culture. After leaving college, Beth had a few relationships and when they ended, she returned to hookup culture via dating apps. It was at this time that Beth realized that she could not get what she was looking for by hooking up.

Sexual desire partially fueled her hookups, but there was always an attendant (but unspoken) hope that the hookup would turn into something more. When it didn't, she felt hopeless, undesirable, and not like "marriage material." It was at this time that Beth decided to stop hooking up and to date only people who were similarly looking for a long-term relationship. Beth opted not to have sex for about a year until she started dating a guy she really liked. They agreed to be exclusive before "consummating" their relationship. Beth honored Her Sexy by identifying that she was not someone who felt emotionally safe having hookup sex. She felt empowered by declaring, without apology or shame, that she needed the relationship first in order to experience all the pleasures of a sexual encounter.

Alana, on the other hand, has had a different relationship with casual sex and has been able to feel empowered and aligned in no-strings attached sex. Alana had a number of casual sexual experiences in college, and she felt clear that the goal of these sexual encounters was pleasure and play. She once had a partner who defined her as his "girlfriend" to his friends before first having a talk with Alana about this shift in motivation. This never sat right with Alana, and she now realizes that is because this partner was trying to define their relationship only in terms of his own motivation without taking Alana's needs and desires into account. Through this relationship, Alana felt she learned a lot about the importance of proactively checking in about her own and her partner's motivations.

Alana is now in her midtwenties. She goes on dates and enjoys casual sex when there is a sexual connection for both parties, a shared agreement on the motivation for the casual sex (desire for sexual pleasure, exploration, and play), a constant check-in of what each partner is feeling toward the relationship, and, of course, a discussion of boundaries and consent. Alana views each casual sexual encounter as an opportunity to learn more about her body and her pleasure, and as an opportunity to explore how to be more mindful and attuned as a lover. Right now, Alana feels that her life is too busy for a deeper, committed relationship, but she also feels like forgoing her sexual pleasure altogether would be a sacrifice of her power as a woman.

Unapologetically Aligned

Pleasure is your sexual birthright, and it can be found in different sexual roles. The stories of Beth and Alana highlight the need to author your own unfolding story, and that what feels uplifting for your best friend might feel awful for you. If you were unpacking this delicious complexity with Alana and Beth (over a cold beer or a hot tea), they would challenge you to be intentional and honest about your wants and needs. Your mind, your body, and your intuition hold infinite wisdom, and your journey through this book will help you tap those sources of power and alignment. From that place of connection to self, it becomes so much easier to talk with a partner about pleasure and about boundaries. As much as we might want our intimate partners to be mind readers, we must bridge the space between us with courageous conversation.

Your Sexy is infused with intuition and a deep faith in yourself. As you deepen your relationship with yourself, you can hear and trust when you come face-to-face with an option that is a "no." That voice becomes clear as a bell, and you can hold your boundary without apology or guilt. That deepened trust in yourself is also what allows you to say a heartfelt "yes" to whatever it is that you desire. Loving is a risk, and heartbreak happens. You can love, lose, grow, and rise from the ashes like a phoenix ready for the next challenge life will bring.

�֍

You will have all kinds of sex in your lifetime, driven by all kinds of desires—aching you feel in your loins, curiosity to try something new, longing for a baby, craving for closeness and connection, need for an escape, relief from a migraine (that works for some people!), or needing sleep (this is true too!). Live in deeper alignment by relating to Your Sexy as an unfolding, imperfect, messy story. The more you trust yourself, the easier it is to tune in to what you want, ask for what you need, and walk away from what isn't working.

mental

6

What You Think Matters

It is the internal transformation that matters most. If there is one
thing that has made a difference in my life, it is the courage to
turn and face what wants to change within me.

—Elizabeth Lesser, *Broken Open*

It's my regular Thursday afternoon office hours, and my student Jo, a
college senior, knocks tentatively on my open door. I invite her in. She
sits nervously on the edge of the chair, fiddling with the zipper on her
backpack.

"What's up?" I ask.

"I want to talk to you about something personal. I'm reading your
book and trying to use your Name-Connect-Choose process to change
how I feel about hooking up. And it's not working. I need you to tell
me what I'm doing wrong!"

I was intrigued and more than a little confused, so I asked her to
tell me more about her situation. Here's what she shared:

"I hate hooking up. But it's all that happens around here, so I'm
trying to get myself to like it. I named that I hate hooking up. It makes
me feel anxious and awful. I connected with the experience of hooking
up and the feelings I have about it. My pattern is this: I drink a lot and
then hook up with a guy. When I get home, I feel like I can't get clean
enough. Wherever he touched me, my lips, my butt, it just feels gross
and like it's not mine, like numb and dirty. But here's where I get stuck.
Even though I'm working so hard to process those feelings, I can't get
past them to choose the thing I want to choose—to be good at hooking
up! I'm frustrated. I want a boyfriend so badly, and this is the only way
to get one. I feel like a failure."

My emotional reaction to Jo's story was pretty intense—feelings of sadness and worry mixed with a sense of real urgency, but I was crystal clear that I wanted to help her Name-Connect-Choose her way into a more inside-out experience of Her Sexy. I wanted her to ground herself in her desires, her boundaries, and her body's data so she could begin to make choices guided by *self-awareness*, not peer pressure or fear.

The third location on our Map of Sexual Self-Awareness is mind, and we will explore how your thoughts, beliefs, and expectations create the conditions for enjoyable sexual experiences or for miserable ones. Mindfulness and self-compassion are amazing tools that help you harness the power of your largest sex organ: your brain!

Not Too Rigid, Not Too Chaotic

We're about to look at why a happy and healthy Sexy requires that we avoid extremes, but first, a quick backstory. Once upon a time, one of my favorite relationship scientists, Dan Siegel, stumbled into a big aha moment while flipping through the DSM (the huge book that therapists use to diagnose mental health problems). He realized that every single disorder in that book could be lumped into one of two broad categories—a disorder of *rigidity* or a disorder of *chaos*. When someone has depression, their mood tends to be low and flat. Depression is a disorder of rigidity. When someone has anorexia nervosa, their eating and weight are micromanaged and rule-bound. Anorexia nervosa is a disorder of rigidity too. At the other extreme are disorders of chaos. Someone with bipolar disorder experiences unstable and unpredictable mood variations. Someone with bulimia nervosa struggles with binging and purging. Both of these mental health problems are disorders of chaos.

Human beings are happiest and healthiest when we occupy a shade of gray between rigidity and chaos. Siegel calls this "integration"—not too much sameness and not too unpredictability—and he envisions integration as a river (see the figure below). One riverbank is rigidity, and one riverbank is chaos. We are our best selves when we can float merrily along the river of integration.

River of Integration

It's not just us as individuals who need integration to be healthy. Our relationships need integration as well. Couples come to me for therapy because their love boat has drifted out of the river and is stuck on either the bank of rigidity or the bank of chaos.

- *Rigid couples* describe feeling bored, disengaged, and stale in the relationship. They feel like the "spark" is gone, and they are usually neglecting romantic and erotic connection.

- *Chaotic couples* describe feeling anxious, angry, afraid, or suspicious. They may be cycling through breakups and reunions, reeling from the reveal of an affair, or struggling with violence and toxic conflict.

The central tension of love is that we want to feel safe but not too safe, excited but not terrified. As Esther Perel says, "Love rests on two pillars: surrender and autonomy. Our need for togetherness exists alongside our need for separateness."[63] Our relationships are happiest and healthiest when we find ways to blend *both* safety *and* novelty.

Your Sexy Craves a Shade of Gray

Your Sexy wants to hang out with you in the river of integration, supported with thoughts, beliefs, and practices that are neither too rigid nor too chaotic. Let's consider what that means. *Sexual rigidity* looks like Your Sexy being constrained by limiting beliefs about yourself or about sex: "sex is sinful/dirty/wrong," "I am sexually broken/deviant/ abnormal," "I am not sexy," or "I am bad at sex." Note that talking about sexual rigidity gets a bit tricky because your sense of right/wrong/ good/bad when it comes to sex may very well have come from a religious institution. Although I have zero interest in getting between you and your relationship with your higher power, I am deeply interested in inviting your awareness to the impact of your tightly held beliefs about sex. To what degree do these beliefs serve your sexual health (body, heart, and soul), and to what degree do they fuel shame, fear, and isolation? We will spend more time at the intersection of sex and spirituality in chapter 10.

Sexual chaos looks like Your Sexy being constrained by underlying beliefs about yourself or about sex that set the stage for reckless, careless, dangerous, or knee-jerk choices about where/when/how you express yourself sexually: "I am not worthy of safe/pleasurable/rewarding sexual experiences," "What happens to me sexually doesn't really matter," or "Sex is no big deal."

Sexual integration is our goal and is characterized in the following ways:

- I relate to my sexual fantasies with curiosity, not fear.

- I am able to tune in to my body during sex.

- I am able to ask for what I need and want during sex.

- I am able to say no when I need to.

- I am aware of the risks of too much sameness and too much unpredictability and have practices that help me cultivate integration.

Nobody is perfect, and we are all at risk of hitting rough sexual waters and crashing onto one of these banks. What's most important is learning to recognize when you are slipping into rigidity or chaos and having tools to move yourself back toward a place of integration.

The table on the next page will help you assess the degree to which you and Your Sexy are splashing around together in this river of integration versus stuck on the riverbank of rigidity or chaos. Notice that there are two columns. The first column, "Internal," captures how sexual rigidity, sexual chaos, and sexual integration look and feel *inside of you.* The second column, "Relational," captures how sexual rigidity, sexual chaos, and sexual integration look and feel in the relationship *between you and a partner.* Look at the first column and answer these questions:

- Where on this table would you locate Your Sexy today?

- Where on this table would you like Your Sexy to be?

- What are the biggest factors that get in the way of integration?

Remember the Golden Equation of Love (my stuff + your stuff = our stuff) as you look at the second column and answer these questions:

- If you are currently in an intimate relationship, how much sexual integration is present? What is getting in the way of sexual integration?

- If you are currently single, think about past relationships. How much sexual integration was present? What got in the way of sexual integration?

	Internal (within me)	**Relational** (between a partner and me)
Sexual Rigidity	I believe sex is sinful. I believe I am bad at sex. I believe I am broken, damaged, or worthless sexually.	We have sex the same way every time. We can't talk about sex. We have stopped having sex. We don't enjoy the sex we have.
Sexual Chaos	I often find myself in sexual situations that are physically or emotionally unsafe. I "check out" during sex.	My relationship is sexually violent. My relationship is sexually neglectful. My relationship has sexual unpredictability that feels stressful rather than pleasurable or playful.
Sexual Integration	I relate to My Sexy with compassion, curiosity, and care. I am able to be mindfully present most of the time during sexual experiences.	We are invested in creating sexual situations that are both safe and playful. Our sexual experiences take both of our needs into account.

Great Sex is Both Within and Between

Sex is about what's going on inside of you *and* what is going on in the space between yourself and your partner. It's another big and important sexual both-and: I am *both* grounded *and* connected. In other words, I am *both* attuned to me *and* open to you. Sexual integration sounds like this: I tune in to and value my internal world, you tune in to and value your internal world, and from that place of awareness, we cocreate a sexual experience!

For some people, the biggest challenge is to be connected—they become so lost in their own world that they struggle to pay attention to how their partner is doing. For other people, the biggest challenge is to be grounded—they struggle to connect with themselves because they are so focused on their partner. Let's focus now on getting grounded (the "within") because it sets the stage for getting connected (the "between"), which we will address more deeply in chapter 9. Plus, given that women are socialized to be caregivers, getting grounded in our own experience tends to be a challenge for us.

Get grounded by paying attention to your thoughts, because the quality of your self-talk profoundly impacts the quality of your sexual experience. How are you "talking" to yourself during your sexual experiences? Mindfulness and self-compassion help us shift from self-critical to self-loving, from worried to relaxed. Let's explore how we can harness their power.

Showing Up for Sex: Mindfulness

These days everyone, from therapists to business leaders to athletes, is obsessed with *mindfulness*. You cannot attend a mental health conference anywhere without finding one or more workshops devoted to mindfulness and the treatment of anything and everything that ails us: mindfulness and eating disorders, mindfulness and addiction, and so on. We are obsessed because mindfulness works. These skills make us healthier, happier, and better able to face the challenges of being human.[64]

Mindfulness is the practice of bringing your attention to the present moment without judgment. Mindfulness is the difference between being enmeshed with your thoughts and noticing, "Ah, I am having a thought." Mindfulness is the difference between being flooded by your emotions and noticing, "Wow, I feel the anger churning in my belly and radiating to the tips of my toes." Mindfulness is the single most powerful tool we can use to move our boat from the bank of rigidity or the bank of chaos back into the river of integration.

The bad news is that mindfulness isn't just a box you check off on your way to greater health. It is a practice, and, as with most things in life, the more we practice, the better we get. The good news is that you have an immense amount of freedom and flexibility about where, when, and how you practice being mindful. You can experiment with mindful walking meditations, mindful eating exercises, mindful breathing meditations, and more!

There are so many great books, audio recordings, and apps devoted to teaching mindfulness, so play around and see what works for you. You may find it helpful to take several brief two- or three-minute *mindfulness breaks* throughout the day, for example when you sit down to a meal, when you park your car at work in the morning, or when you are in the shower. Or you might enjoy doing one longer daily mindfulness meditation.

Mindfulness meditations take practice, but the benefits to your physical and emotional well-being are worth it. Mindfulness practices have been linked to reduced rumination, stress reduction, boosts to working memory, improved focus, less emotional reactivity, more flexible thinking, greater relationship satisfaction, greater self-insight, heightened intuition, increased immune functioning, greater well-being, less psychological distress, less task effort, and fewer thoughts unrelated to the task at hand.[65]

Pleasure is embodied. Pleasurable sex rests, in part, on our ability to be mindful—firmly, steadily, and fully present. In fact, researcher Lori Brotto and her team have found that mindfulness practices significantly improve sexual desire for women.[66] For some women, this is easy. The world fades away, the mind quiets, and they relish the five-sensory journey offered via sex.

For a lot of women, mindfulness during sex is a tall order. The intense physical and emotional vulnerability of sex can evoke thoughts and feelings that move us away from the pleasures of the present moment. Barriers to mindfulness are, unfortunately, practically limitless and may include:

- worries about how your partner is feeling (physically, emotionally, both)

- anxiety about how this sexual experience will affect your relationship

- self-critical thoughts about your body

- shame-loaded thoughts about sex as sinful/bad/wrong

- emotionally charged flashbacks from prior traumatic experiences

- thoughts about work, family stress, chores, the to-do list, and so forth

- distraction or numbness because of the effects of drugs or alcohol (which may have been used in the first place in an effort to quiet down the impact of the rest of these distractors!).

Here's a particularly heartbreaking barrier to mindful sex. Researchers have found that about half of women who have sex with men persist through painful sex.[67] Further, women often report faking an orgasm to end painful sex in a way that doesn't threaten their partner's identity or provoke anger or conflict.[68] *Pain during sex is an indication that you and your partner need to do something differently.* Perhaps you and your partner need to use lubrication. Perhaps you need more kissing, caressing, manual penetration, and/or oral sex before you have penile-vaginal intercourse. Perhaps your partner is doing some stuff that seems possible in porn but painful in real life (like deep and vigorous thrusting). Perhaps you need to consult with your doctor about an undiagnosed medical problem. Painful sex and mindful sex cannot coexist, and your pain deserves your (and your partner's) attention.

If you struggle with mindfulness during sex, please resist the urge to create a good-bad or right-wrong split inside of your head right now. Do not simplify this and start down a path of saying that you're doing sex "wrong" because you struggle to feel at home in your body during sex. And please do not imagine that full 100 percent mindfulness is a place of nirvana at which you will arrive if you work hard enough. Instead, just bring your awareness to the question, *"What keeps me from being present during sex?"* Naming the doors through which you exit presence during sex is the first step toward figuring out what would help you stay in the room. This isn't easy. It's a journey. You have time. Be nice to you!

Maybe you already have a mindfulness practice that you love. If not, commit yourself to trying this simple mindfulness practice for at least five minutes each day for a week. Notice how you feel before, during, and after the practice each day. Notice also how you feel at the end of the seven days of practice.

- Sit comfortably.

- As you sit, still and quiet, scan your body, bringing your attention to each part, from head to toes. Take note of the various sensations you are experiencing.

- Focus on your breath, noticing how it feels in your nose, mouth, chest, and belly.

- As thoughts bounce around inside your head, return your focus to your breath. This will happen many times. Imagine that your present-moment awareness is a blue sky and each thought inside your head is a cloud. When a thought comes in, note it and allow it to pass on by like a cloud, returning your attention to the sky—your present-moment awareness of your breath. You will need to do this over and over again before it starts to feel natural.

No Enemies Within: Self-Compassion

Speaking of being nice to you, let's talk about the other tool we can use to navigate the mental aspect of sex: self-compassion. Kristin Neff, the leading researcher in this area, explains that self-compassion has three components:[69]

Self-kindness. "Self-compassion entails being warm and understanding toward ourselves when we suffer, fail, or feel inadequate, rather than ignoring our pain or flagellating ourselves with self-criticism."[70]

Common humanity. Being compassionate with ourselves involves recognizing that suffering and personal inadequacy are part of the shared human experience. Shame says, "I am the only one who feels like this." Self-compassion says, "Everyone screws up or feels lousy from time to time."

Mindfulness. We defined mindfulness above. When we are mindful, we bring our attention into the present moment (neither fast-forwarding to an imagined catastrophic future nor rewinding to old stories about the past), and we adopt a nonjudgmental and receptive state of mind in which we observe our thoughts and feelings rather than trying to suppress or deny them. Mindfulness is the difference between thinking, *I'm not sexy*, and thinking, *Oh, here comes that old, played-out story about how I am not sexy. I will be compassionate with myself in the face of this story.*

Self-compassion is different from self-esteem. It's not about hollowly propping yourself up or mindlessly offering yourself affirmations about your awesomeness. Self-compassion is also not about letting yourself off the hook. It is about embracing your imperfections and making a commitment to be gentle with yourself.

You have a conversation going inside of your head all day long. We all do! Think about your inner voice like an announcer at a sporting event providing "color commentary" as you go about the business of being you. We self-narrate as we move through our days. The fact that we do this is neither a good thing nor a bad thing, but it is a thing that begs the question: *What is the quality of the conversation that you are having with yourself?* It is worth exploring how kind that voice inside your head is. Because we are inherently relational, we talk to ourselves the way we were talked to. For better or worse, the voice inside your head was forged in part by the relationships you had when you were young.

Self-compassion is ultimately about treating yourself the way you would treat a good friend. For most of us, it is second nature to relate to a good friend with compassion, meeting their distress with our patience, celebrating their accomplishments with our validation, and greeting their mere existence with our love. Don't you deserve the very same in your relationship with yourself?

Your Sexy needs and deserves nothing less than your radical self-compassion in bed. Practicing self-compassion may be just what the doctor ordered if you find yourself doing any or all of the following:

- Spectatoring: watching yourself during sex instead of being immersed in the experience

- Judging how you're "doing" instead of how you're feeling

- Judging your body's shape or size, how you smell, or the sounds you make as you orgasm.

Your relationship with Your Sexy is wonderful and tough and complicated, and you are so much better positioned to meet all that messiness when you have yourself on your own team! The payoffs for being self-compassionate with Your Sexy extend to your life outside of the bedroom as well. Because self-compassion helps us feel more at home in our own skin, your commitment to self-compassion will help you build relationships with people and feel more confident, open to possibilities, and resilient in the face of challenges.

Reflect on or write about these questions:

- How self-compassionate are you?

- What blocks your ability (or willingness) to be self-compassionate?

- What helps you feel more self-compassionate?

From Regret to FGO

We know by now that the journey toward greater sexual self-awareness requires self-compassion. As Maya Angelou said, "Do the best you can until you know better. Then when you know better, do better."[71] The story of Your Sexy may have a chapter or two that you wish you could delete altogether. The story of a sexual trauma is for sure an example, but that's not what I mean here. Here, I just mean sexual experiences that you recall with a tinge of shame, embarrassment, ick, or regret.

These stories, when they remain charged with the energy of regret, threaten to cast a shadow that dulls the brilliance of Your Sexy. Reframe those unfortunate stories by thinking of them as FGOs— fucking growth opportunities. From the biggest, widest perspective, that lousy and inattentive lover, for example, was your teacher. That lousy lover has given you the opportunity to learn about what you need in place in order to enjoy sex. The question becomes: *What will you do with this FGO?* You deserve to integrate the FGO into your story, using it as a lesson about what you need going forward in order to live in alignment with your sexual self. Sexual self-awareness is about trusting the wisdom of your data, which come in many forms. An FGO is a kind of data that helps you learn what you need so that you can make new choices going forward.

Remember Jo from the beginning of this chapter, who wanted to learn to love hooking up? I wanted her to connect with the power of her body's data so her lousy hookups could become FGOs. I asked Jo what might shift for her if she began to trust the data that her body was so clearly providing her with. She was using the Name-Connect-Choose process to try to get better at hooking up because of her limiting belief that hooking up is the only pathway to a romantic relationship. We worked together to use the Name-Connect-Choose process in a *different* way. I reflected to her the wisdom of her body, saying, "Jo, your body is brilliant! Not being able to feel your lips or your booty the next day is crystal-clear data. Let's see what happens if we work *with* your body's data instead of *against* it." Here's what we came up with:

Name. I hate hooking up. I find it gross. I do it because I want a boyfriend, and I feel like this is the only way I can get one.

Connect. When I get drunk and hook up with someone I just met, I feel anxious and insecure *before*, I feel upset *during*, and I feel numb, dirty, and sad *after*. As I sit with these feelings, I feel sad and stuck.

Choose. Hooking up does not work for me.

Helping her get to the sexually self-aware "Choose" of ending the hookup cycle was a bit challenging. As an ambitious and brilliant young woman, she hated feeling like a failure, and her story about hooking up was that she was falling behind her peers. Historically, trying harder yielded success, so shifting her mindset was not easy. Trusting her body's data felt to her like giving up, like letting herself off the hook. I let her know that research indicates that a lot of people feel the same way she does about hooking up.[72] She's far from alone in wanting to start a romantic relationship in a different way—going on a date, developing a friendship first, and so on. I encouraged her to *be* the change she wants to see in the relationship world!

By harnessing the power of sexual self-awareness, you create the sexual experiences that feel sexy from the *inside-out*. I am not even focusing necessarily on you having an orgasm. Rather, I am inviting you to embrace the fact that you are entitled to sexual experiences that enhance you. Experiences that leave you feeling more alive, more connected (to yourself and to your partner), more curious. If you walk away from a sexual experience feeling diminished, numb, ashamed, or alone, it is vital for you to pay attention. Those feelings are data. Those feelings are information. Do not let yourself get stuck, creating for yourself the story: "This must be what sex is all about." Instead, take those data and talk to yourself about them: "Ah! I do not like the way I am feeling now. The way I am feeling now lets me know that I need to find a different way going forward." Eff yeah for FGOs.

Reflect on your sexual experiences to this point and see whether you meet up with a memory that is tinged with shame, embarrassment, or regret. Write responsively to these questions:

- What did you learn from the experience?

- What do you do differently now because of what you learned from that experience?

- What happens inside if you reframe that experience as an FGO? Do you notice a shift?

Before you move on, put your hand on your heart, take some deep breaths, and send yourself some unconditional love. That's self-compassion in action.

The Mantra That Your Sexy Deserves

I love a good mantra—strong and clear words you can use to get you "in the zone." I want to offer a mantra that I think Your Sexy is really going to love! Ready for it?

I enter into a sexual experience if, and only if, my pleasure and my safety are central features of the experience.

This mantra may feel like a revelation to you. Or it may feel like a yawn because you've been abiding by it for years. If the latter is the case, brava to you! You are channeling some serious divine feminine power, inviting yourself and your partner(s) into greater awareness and healing. Keep up the great work! If this mantra feels brand new to you, go slowly. Walk around in this mantra like it's a new pair of shoes. Settle in. Notice your resistance—the parts of you that are saying, "yes…but…"

One of the women I spoke with for this book, Renee, feels like she is beginning to embrace this mantra. Renee went to college without a clear sense of what sex even was and didn't have much sexual experience until the end of college. In all of her sexual experiences in her early twenties, her male partners would take the lead, and she would lie still and make the noises she had seen women in porn make. She faked orgasms 100 percent of the time, not consciously to spare her partner's ego but simply because she had no conceptualization that her pleasure was a possibility. She recounted to me that she would "code" her sexual experiences in one of two ways: good or bad. A good experience was pain-free and involved snuggling after. A bad experience was physically painful and snuggle-free, leaving her feeling lonely and discouraged.

Renee experienced a massive paradigm shift when she started, for the first time ever, to talk with her friends about sex. Over brunch, they would compare and contrast their sexual experiences, and this provided Renee with long overdue validation and education. Through these conversations, she got clear that she needed and deserved to up-level her sexual expectations. Her former "ceiling" (good sex as pain-free and snuggly) became her new "floor." She now enters into her sexual experiences expecting that both she and her partner will attend to her pleasure. She also has stopped having nonrelationship sex because she realized that romantic love and emotional intimacy are essential for activating her sexual accelerator and for helping her feel safe enough that she can let go and be mindful.

Mindfulness and self-compassion are key practices for great sex, helping you flow with (rather than fight against) your brain. Tuning in to your internal conversation—and making sure you're speaking to yourself with kindness and love—will help you sit more comfortably with the messy contradictions of Your Sexy. You are a feminist who is massively turned on by a fantasy about being ravished by a man who can't control himself around you? Drop any judgment you may want to make and remember that Your Sexy is a place of great paradox and mystery. You are a new parent who can't imagine feeling sexy ever again? Let go of expectation and trust that the story of your sexuality has many chapters. Your Sexy deserves your patience (and your partner's patience too). As you begin to spend more time in the river of integration (and less time stuck on the shore), you will relate to Your Sexy with more acceptance and affirmation. Shifting out of rigid notions of who and how you should be sexually and into a gentle curious stance vis-à-vis Your Sexy will guide you to sexual experiences that hold the power to enliven, connect, and heal you.

✳

We are happiest and healthiest in our lives when we inhabit a shade of gray between rigidity and chaos. Too much same and we feel bored and flat. Too much variability and we feel out of control and unsafe. Your Sexy is like Goldilocks, seeking out that "just right" place so that she can unfurl and enjoy. And to do that, you need to harness the power of your mind through mindfulness and self-compassion.

physical

7

It's Time to Be Sweet to All of You

Treat cultural messages about sex and your body like a salad bar. Take only the things that appeal to you and ignore the rest. We'll all end up with a different collection of stuff on our plates, but that's how it's supposed to work. It goes wrong only when you try to apply what you picked as right for your sexuality to someone else's sexuality.

—Emily Nagoski, *Come as You Are*

Anjali is a twenty-seven-year-old Italian American woman who just ended a four-year relationship and is cautiously and courageously reentering the dating world. Anjali is also gorgeous—like take-your-breath-away, supermodel beautiful. What's less-than-beautiful however is the current state of her relationship with her lady parts. In fact, she and her vulva are struggling big time! When she was in a long-term relationship, her personal grooming routine was simple. She would shave her bikini line and trim the rest of her pubic hair. As she started to date again after the breakup, this routine suddenly felt inadequate. Imagining getting naked with a new partner made her feel understandably anxious. Instead of DIY "ladyscaping," she started to have all her hair waxed off by a professional...for a pretty penny!

Her body-hair maintenance is none of anyone's business, but we can learn from the story that was driving her choice—her *why*. Anjali told me about the thinking process that drove her decision to wax: "I feel like I am in competition with all of these other women, and I want to present myself in the best possible light." Anjali is a good student, right? She has been paying attention to the lessons that her culture has been telling her for years: women need to compete with other women for the scarce and valuable resource of male attention.

Her fear-driven scramble to feel worthy was relentless. As it turned out, being hair-free did not fix her fear that she would not measure up down there. Instead, it exposed a brand-new body image concern—one that had been previously hidden. Anjali started to feel like her labia were the wrong color. So, she started to research "vaginal bleaching."[73] Until her best friend and roommate sat her down and gave her a talk entitled, "Any man who judges you for the color of your labia does not deserve to be anywhere near that precious thing!" I feel clear that everyone needs a friend like that!

Notice the thoughts and feelings that stir in you as you read Anjali's story. Are you feeling tempted to judge her as neurotic or insecure? Are you feeling validated because you've had these insecurities as well? Are you feeling pissed off that we live in a world in which beauty standards shape our relationship with even our most intimate area? Just notice those thoughts and feelings because they point your awareness in an essential direction—toward the relationship between your body and Your Sexy. In this chapter, we will unpack how your relationship with your body shapes what you feel able to ask for, receive, and enjoy sexually.

Who Profits from That Negative Thought?

The pressure on women to be thin/fit/flawless can feel crushing. Renee Engeln studies women and body image and how an extreme focus on appearance compromises our physical and emotional well-being. She writes about how girls and women get trapped in this wretched Catch-22. We are taught from an early age that we need to be perceived as beautiful in order to belong, but then, when we focus on our appearance, we are judged (sometimes by other girls and women) as being "superficial."[74] Talk about a no-win game! As women, we live in a world that feels fully justified in judging and assessing our physical appearance and are encouraged to place much of our self-worth in how favorably we are "scored" on a set of criteria we didn't create.

Entire industries have been built upon the story that women need to be beautiful in order to be worthy. When you find yourself traveling down that rabbit hole of negative body image, stop and ask yourself, *"Who is profiting off of my negative thoughts?"* This gut check can help you turn self-deprecation into feistiness and remind you that it is revolutionary to love yourself as you are. As feminist author Audre Lorde states, "Caring for myself is not self-indulgence. It is self-preservation, and that is an act of political warfare."[75]

Yes, men also feel pressure to conform to beauty standards like broad shoulders, six-pack abs, narrow waists, and large penises, but there tend to be two major gender differences. First, men tend to evaluate their bodies in a holistic way, considering their bodies as one entire unit. Women tend to evaluate their bodies as a "series of pull-apart components that need to be altered or fixed."[76] Exhibit A: Anjali labeling her vulva ugly. Second, men tend to think about their body's capability, and women tend to think about their body as something to be looked at and scrutinized.[77] It is a distinction between feeling like a "subject" (someone who does something) and feeling like an "object" (a thing that others gaze upon, evaluate, and act upon). This is why street harassment and catcalling are so pernicious. Even if a woman doesn't feel deeply afraid for her safety when a stranger whistles at her or tells her to smile, this moment serves as a reminder that her body is the object of evaluation wherever she goes.

Remember chapter 4, where we discussed that any feminist critique must be intersectional in nature. Gender is a rather unhelpful stand-alone category, as research indicates that the more marginalized identities you belong to, the greater risk you carry of being at war with your own body. Research indicates that gay men are at greater risk of body image concerns and eating disorders than men who identify as heterosexual. People who are both LGBTQ+ and nonwhite have an equivalent or higher prevalence of eating disorders when compared with people who are LGBTQ+ and white. Importantly, people who feel *connected to* the LGBTQ+ community are at lower risk of eating disorders than those without a sense of belonging.[78] Communities create a powerful bridge between the *me* and the *we*. Shame cannot survive the warm glow of connection. It is much harder to do battle against yourself when you have opportunities to look deeply into the eyes of people who are like you and people who like you. Feeling part of a collective helps you push back against toxic cultural stories that dehumanize you and delegitimize your very existence. And feeling at peace in your skin is the foundation for experiencing pleasure of all kinds, including sexual pleasure.

Reclamation Demands Body Love

When I start thinking about how cultural standards of beauty set the stage for women to struggle with body image problems and feelings of inadequacy, I can get pretty rage-y pretty quickly. I crave a massive cultural overhaul, one that frees us up to fully inhabit our bodies, celebrating every inch of us exactly as we are. In the meantime, as we work toward that vision, let's commit to practices that can make a difference in our own lives and in the lives of the girls and women we love, including:

> **Emphasize other priorities.** Think of time and energy as a pie that gets divided up into all of the pieces of your life. The things you do to maintain or improve your appearance are a piece of the pie. How big a piece of the pie is your appearance right now? Are there aspects of yourself that are neglected because you are investing in your appearance?

> **Resist the urge to compare yourself to others.** As Brené Brown says, "Stay in your lane. Comparison kills creativity and joy."[79] When you notice yourself feeling envious about how someone else looks, that's your cue that you're out of "your lane." In that moment, take a deep breath, put your hand on your heart, and send yourself some love. While you're at it, send the object of your envy some love too, trusting there is plenty of good stuff to go around.

Eliminate fat talk. It is an unfortunate reality that women sometimes engage each other in self-deprecating body talk, and the focus is frequently about feeling fat or wanting to lose weight. Even seemingly benign comments like, "I don't deserve a snack today because I didn't work out," or "I gained so much weight over the holidays," reinforce this idea that our bodies are constant projects and that our self-worth is at least in part dictated by the number on the scale. See if you can eliminate or reduce the amount of fat talk that happens inside of your head. When you let your friends know that you're not down for that conversation, everyone wins.

Limit image-focused social media consumption. Social media is neither a "good thing" nor a "bad thing." It's way more complicated than that. But lots of us are spending more time than we need scrolling through social media accounts featuring highly curated and filtered images. As author Steven Furtick says, "The reason we struggle with insecurity is because we compare our behind-the-scenes with everyone else's highlight reel."[80] Research has found that spending time looking at highly visual social media has a clear detrimental effect on body image.[81] Start to cue in to how you feel before, during, and after you spend time looking at these image-focused accounts.

Fuel your workouts with gratitude. Your workout can be energized with the power of fear, or it can be energized with the power of love. You know your workout is powered by fear if your motivating thoughts sound like this: *If you don't go, you're going to gain weight,* and *You need to get in shape for the summer.* By contrast, you know that your workout is powered by love if you choose exercises that you enjoy and motivate yourself with thoughts that sound more like this: *You're going to feel so good when you're done,* and *You deserve some time to celebrate how good it feels to move your body.*

We will end this section with these words from poet Hollie Holden:

Could You Just Love Me Like This

Today I asked my body what she needed...
Which is a big deal,
Considering my journey of
Not really asking that much.

I thought she might need more water.
Or protein.
Or greens.
Or yoga.
Or supplements.
Or movement.

But as I stood in the shower
Reflecting on her stretch marks,
Her roundness where I would like flatness,
Her softness where I would like firmness,
All those conditioned wishes
That form a bundle of
Never-Quite-Right-Ness,
She whispered very gently:

Could you just love me like this?

Couples Therapy for You and Your Vulva

So far, we have looked at how cultural stories tie our appearance to our worth, but let's get more specific, because body image and sexuality are so entwined. *How is the relationship between you and your vulva?* If you're like a lot of women, that relationship is a bit strained. You may not know "her" very well, and you may not be loving her the way she wants and needs to be loved. Because sexual self-awareness is about integrating the thoughts, feelings, beliefs, and stories you carry inside of you, it's vital to attend to your story of your vulva. As we saw with Anjali, that story can be quite self-critical. Body-related shame and insecurity can be most intense in relation to our most intimate areas.

Often, this shame is woven into the language we use to talk about our intimate areas—or to not talk about them, as the case may be. Years ago, I was at a bachelorette party in New York City for a friend from grad school. We were sitting around a table at a bar, and the conversation turned to lady parts. Specifically, we started talking about what we called our vulvas in our families growing up. The group was roaring with laughter as women started sharing all the funny names—sissy, chi-chi, hoo-hoo. Then I chimed in, "Oh I know one! The front butt." In my memory, it was like that scene in the movies where the record scratches to a halt, the room goes quiet, all you can hear is the ticking of a clock, and everyone is staring at the person who just made a gaffe. Years later, I think this story is hilarious, but at the time I felt super embarrassed and exposed. There's so much power in a name. Language shapes experience.

As Dumbledore tells Harry, "Call him Voldemort, Harry. Always use the proper name for things. Fear of a name increases fear of the thing itself."[82] So, what keeps us from using the proper names for our genitals? Shame? Sure. A cultural story that if you know a lot about sex, it means you're a whore (and therefore worthless)? Sure. But there's a simple answer too. Many of us can't use proper names because we don't know them. Female genitalia are physically shrouded. By design, it can be a bit tricky to see and explore our "down theres"—trickier certainly than it is for a guy to see and explore his. Our genitals are emotionally shrouded too—by stories that shame girls and women for their curiosity. We tend to be much more permission-giving when it comes to boys' fascination with their penises than we are about girls' fascination with their vulva. This tendency is rooted, no doubt, in our overall struggle to reconcile female pleasure. For trans folks, and those whose genitalia do not fit neatly into a gender binary, shame can be a massive barrier to pleasure and body love as well.

Where does this leave us? With a whole lot of us feeling like our genitalia are a mystery...and less of a wonderfully adventurous Holy-Grail-Da-Vinci-Code-Hope-Diamond kind of mystery...more of an I'm-a-bad-dirty-person-for-wanting-to-understand kind of mystery. *We cannot get answers to questions that we are too ashamed to ask.* Kristen, a twenty-two-year-old nurse, shared with me, "I remember being in my first year of nursing school and learning all of the parts of the female genitalia. I was so pissed! I thought my high school had done a decent job with sex education. So why did I have to be in nursing school before I could name the parts of my own body?!" Our education is often limited to identifying the reproductive system (ovaries, fallopian tubes, and the uterus), omitting the external genitalia. This omission reinforces the idea that the only function of a woman's body is to carry a baby, not to be sexual. The void left by this omission is readily filled with the shame of what then ends up feeling unspeakable.

When shown a diagram of the external female genitalia, only about half of female college students and only about one quarter of male college students could correctly identify over 80 percent of the anatomical structures.[83] Far from a purely academic exercise, there are real-life consequences for a lack of intimate knowledge about a woman's intimate parts. How can an intimate partner, especially if that partner doesn't share the same parts, connect competently or confidently with a body they don't understand? How can a woman be expected to advocate for her sexual wants, needs, and desires without an owner's manual? Research indicates that carrying negative feelings about your vulva is associated with lower self-esteem, less sexual satisfaction, and riskier sexual behavior.[84]

I want to be crystal clear. Picking up a negative feeling or two about your genitals in this culture of ours is 100 percent understandable.

- Companies make millions on feminine deodorant products because there's a deeply misguided notion that vulva are inherently dirty and smelly. (Side note: If you are experiencing a foul odor, do not head to the drugstore for a spray or a wash. Head to your doctor's office.)

- Some of the nastiest names you can call somebody are words also used to describe our genitals (pussy, cunt) or names of products for our genitals (douchebag) or just weird made-up words that relate to our genitals (like a man calling another man a "mangina"). Seriously, dude? A vagina was literally your doorway into this world. That passageway deserves nothing less than your total and complete reverence, thank you very much!

Carrying a belief that your vulva is weird, ugly, dirty, bad, or wrong is understandable given how our culture actively perpetuates that story. We can use our Name-Connect-Choose process to push back against this story and shift from shame to pride. We are going to *name* our parts. Then we'll *connect* with the emotions we carry in relation to those parts, shedding judgment and claiming respect. From that place of awareness and gentleness, we can *choose* a more affirming relationship with our vulva.

Anatomy 101: Where Your Wild Things Are

Let's take a look "under the hood." The first thing you need to know is that women's bodies are wildly diverse, especially our external genitalia. Sex educator Emily Nagoski writes, "We're all made of the same parts, but in each of us, those parts are organized in a unique way that changes over our life-span."[85] As you look at the diagrams, you may start to focus on the degree to which your body does or does not look like them. If you find yourself slipping into comparison and judgment, there are two things you must do immediately:

1. Read the quote from Nagoski again. We are all normal, and no two of us are alike. Your vulva is a snowflake, my dear.

2. Google "Great Wall of Vagina." The *Great Wall of Vagina* is a series of four hundred plaster casts of the vulvas of women ages eighteen to seventy-six. Described as the "vagina monologues of sculpture," it was created by English artist Jamie

McCartney because "for many women, their genital appearance is a source of anxiety, and I was in a unique position to do something about that."[86] This piece of art reminds us that our definition of "normal" needs to be generous and gentle.

The first diagram below is of the *female reproductive system*, and it is probably very familiar to you from sex ed and biology classes. You can see the ovaries, the fallopian tubes, the uterus, the cervix, and the vagina.[87] Awesome! Yay, reproductive system. You're phenomenal and fabulous. You make all of the people. And we are moving on.

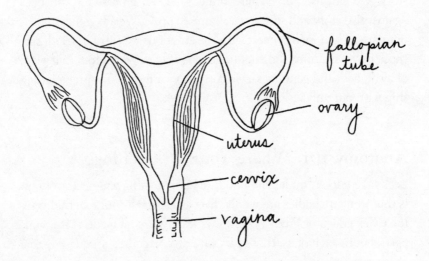

Female Reproductive System

The next diagram is of the *female external genitalia*. This is the one that trips up more than half of the population, and therefore warrants our deeper attention. Let's review what's in this diagram.

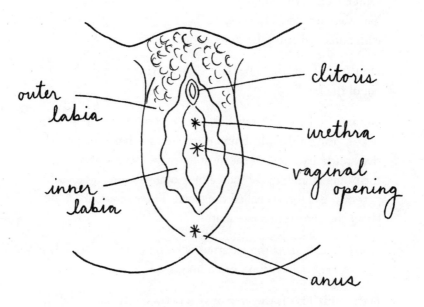

Female External Genitalia

Vulva. The entire external female genitalia including the inner labia, the outer labia, the clitoris, and the opening of the vagina.

Vagina. This is the elastic, muscular canal that connects the uterus with the outside world. The vagina is the part inside of you. Menstrual blood and babies pass through the vagina. Penises, dildos, and fingers are inserted into the vagina during sex.

Inner labia. Also known as the labia minora, the inner labia are the flaps of skin on either side of the vaginal opening.

Outer labia. Also known as the labia majora, the outer labia have two surfaces. The outer surface is pigmented and covered with pubic hair, and the inner surface is smooth.

Urethra. This is the tube that conveys urine from the bladder out of the body.

Clitoris. This is the sensitive and erectile organ that lives next to the urethra. In humans, the clitoris has no reproductive or urinary role. It is the most sensitive erogenous zone and the primary anatomical source of sexual pleasure. The visible part of the clitoris is called the glans. There's more to discuss about the clitoris in a moment.

Anus. The anus is the external opening of the rectum. It is also an area rich with nerve endings.

Perineum. This is the area of skin between the anus and the vulva. It is also rich with nerve endings.

Before we move on to the third diagram, let's talk about the labia for a moment. Thanks, at least in part, to the advent of 24-7 free streaming porn, more women than ever before are undergoing plastic surgery in order to create a "designer vagina."[88] This procedure reduces the size of the labia minora in an effort to fit an aesthetic commonly seen in porn.

Feminist groups like Courageous Cunts are pushing back against this trend, and the slogans they use in their "Muff Marches" (that's what they are called!) are nothing short of fabulous: "There's nothing finer than my vagina," "Love your labia," and "Keep your mitts off our bits." I try hard to avoid judging women for personal choices, especially around appearance, but this trend of genital plastic surgery troubles and exhausts me. It feels like yet another way that women scramble to "fix" what is not broken in order to be deemed sexy enough in someone else's gaze. Still, I know that many women feel this is a choice *they* are making with *their* bodies, and that is what bodily autonomy is all about, which is why I want to tread carefully.

It is certainly understandable that a woman would feel sexier when her genitals conform to what is portrayed as ideal or beautiful. And in a world with unrelenting messages tying appearance to worthiness, how might we begin to discern between that which we *authentically* want and that which we think we *should* want because it's what we've been told is beautiful? I go back to our distinction between fear and love. Fear says, "We must all be the same in order to be worthy." Love says, "You are gorgeous and whole as you are, and the celebration of being in your own skin is sexy AF!"

Moving on to the clitoris. The diagram below shows the *full anatomy of the clitoris*. A review of anatomy texts from the nineteenth and twentieth centuries indicates that the clitoris was frequently omitted from diagrams.[89] Get your mind around that for a moment. An entire anatomical structure was omitted from medical texts. Suspicious, yes? We omit that which we don't want to have to deal with, that which terrifies us, that which threatens to shake up the order of things. When the clitoris was included, it was considered a little button above the urethra.[90] Helen O'Connell, who first broke ground in the 1990s by becoming Australia's first female urologist, broke ground again when she published the first complete findings on the full anatomy of the clitoris...in June of 1998.[91]

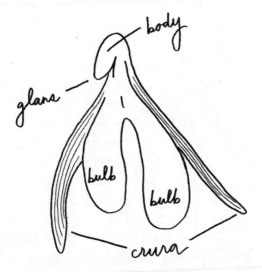

Clitoris

For so long, the clitoris has been written out of our cultural scripts for sex and pleasure. Those in power have attempted to control, minimize, and wholly eliminate the existence of women's sexual pleasure by giving women these messages: your sexuality is for reproductive purposes only, pleasure is solely the domain of men, and your worthiness as women rests upon you being as passive and chaste as possible. We are finally beginning to rewrite the story of women's sexuality, and essential in that process is giving the clit the respect "she" so richly deserves!

Knowledge is power, so here's the scoop. You may remember from your biology class that about six weeks into the development of the embryo, there is a masculinizing hormone wash. If the embryo has XY chromosomes, it responds to the hormone wash and begins to develop a penis, testicles, and scrotum. If the embryo has XX chromosomes, it does not respond to these hormones, and instead develops a clitoris, ovaries, and labia. The clitoris and the penis are the sex organs that are most densely packed with nerve endings. Nagoski says of the clitoris, "Averaging just one-eighth the size of a penis yet loaded with nearly double the nerve endings, it can range in size from a barely visible pea to a fair-sized gherkin, or anywhere in between, and it's all normal, all beautiful."[92] But when it comes to this "love button," there's more than meets the eye.

The glans clitoris and the clitoral hood are visible, as they are on the outside of your body. The body of the clitoris is connected to the glans clitoris. It extends upward into your pelvis and attaches to your pubic bone with ligaments. From the body, the clitoris splits to form the crura and the bulbs. The crura are the "legs" of the clitoris. The bulbs extend through and behind the labia and pass the urethra and vagina toward the anus. Both the crura and the bulbs contain erectile tissue that swells on either side of the vaginal canal during arousal. In fact, these parts can become three times larger during arousal!

The glans clitoris is the only part of the clitoris that does not grow or swell as part of the sexual response. It does not contain erectile (expandable) tissue. The clitoral hood is a fold of skin that is formed by the two sides of the connecting labia minora and is homologous with the foreskin in male genitals. It surrounds and provides protection to the super sensitive glans clitoris, and the clitoral hood is also an erogenous zone. The glans clitoris is a powerhouse of pleasure, home to eight thousand nerve endings. Its only function is to detect sensation and stimulation. Do you hear that, ladies? You have a sex organ whose only function is to help you feel good. Penises multitask: urination, sensation, penetration, and ejaculation. Clitorises have zero effs to give about anything besides feeling good. Let in the awareness that your body is designed for pleasure. *Pleasure is quite literally your birthright.*

Looking at our anatomy, it makes total sense that most women require something besides penetrative sex to experience an orgasm, and we have data to back this up. Take, for example, a recent study with over one thousand women, eighteen to ninety-four years old. (Side note: If your life goal isn't to someday be a great-grandma who tells researchers what gets her off, it really should be!) Less than 20 percent of the women who were having penile-vaginal intercourse experienced an orgasm from intercourse alone; 36.6 percent reported that clitoral stimulation was necessary for orgasm during intercourse, and an additional 36 percent said that although clitoral stimulation was not needed, their orgasms felt better if their clitoris was stimulated during intercourse. The remaining 9 percent either didn't have an orgasm from intercourse or they had an orgasm via cunnilingus or manual stimulation before intercourse happened.[93]

You deserve a gentle and positive connection with your body and its capacity for pleasure. If you have been carrying a story that you are "just not a sexual person," you deserve time and space to unpack and clarify the factors underlying that belief. One possibility is this is your deepest truth, to your very core. Asexuality most certainly exists as a way of being in the world.[94] Another possibility is that it's difficult, if not impossible, to connect with your sexuality if you are unfamiliar and uncomfortable with the body you inhabit. With increased knowledge and comfort, you can advocate for what you want and need sexually. Moving from mystery to mastery of your entire body matters, and it matters a lot.

It is time for a little bit of couples therapy for you and your vulva so that precious relationship is as loving as it can be. Your journey is yours and yours alone, so you get to figure out where the outer edge of your comfort is. You get to create a manageable and meaningful amount of challenge and growth for yourself. Your sweet spot might be determined within the matrix of your culture identities. If your system of culture or spiritual beliefs keep you from trying any of these practices, I invite you to consider how you might be able to move from mystery to mastery in a way that feels consistent with your belief system.

Mindful meditation with the diagrams. Close your eyes and quiet your mind. Focus on your breathing. When you are ready, open your eyes and gaze at the three diagrams from the previous pages. Notice the thoughts and feelings that arise in you as you look at these images. If the thought that arises is a critical or judgmental one (*This is gross*, or *Looking at these is weird*), notice that. Then, see if you can replace that critical thought with a positive one (*Our bodies are beautiful*, or *I am moving toward self-love and wholeness*). Pay attention to your feelings as well. If the feelings that arise are negative (anxiety, shame, sadness), notice that. Then, see if you can meet that negative feeling with something positive and gentle like compassion, pride, or grace. See if the negative feeling lessens or softens as you work on this.

Mindful meditation while using a mirror to look at your vulva. When you feel ready, the next step is to get familiar with *your* vulva. If you have never done this, take your time and set the space. Candles, soft music, and a comfy space could help you prepare for this sacred exploration. All you will need is enough lighting and a small mirror. If you have done this before, you might find it helpful to refresh your memory! Close your eyes and quiet your mind. Focus on your breathing. When you are ready, open your eyes and position the mirror so that you can look at your vulva. Notice the thoughts and feelings that arise in you as you look at yourself. If the thought that arises is a critical or judgmental one (*This is a weird thing to do*, or *I look gross*), just notice that. Then, see if you can meet that critical thought with a positive one (*My body is perfect as it is, I am entitled to understanding all of me*, or *This is mine*). Pay attention to your feelings as well. If the feelings that arise are negative (anxiety, shame, sadness), notice that. Then, see if you can meet that negative feeling with something positive and gentle, like compassion, pride, or grace. See if the negative feeling lessens or softens as you work on this. If you find that you are really struggling with self-criticism, stop and come back to it again. With practice, you will be able to move from self-criticism to self-acceptance, and your effort will be worth it!

Affirmations for all of you. Affirmations are intentional thoughts intended to help you shift from judgment to compassion. Develop a practice of affirmations about your body and see what happens as you do. Try looking at yourself in the mirror and saying something like, "You are beautiful!" or "I adore you!" Try giving yourself some compliments about your body: "My ass looks great in these jeans!" or "My skin is glowing today." Include your vulva in your practice of affirmations. Regena Thomashauer, author of *Pussy: A Reclamation*, says that pussies love attention. Try wishing your vulva good morning. Tell your vulva that she's beautiful and powerful…and yours!

Do You Do Pleasure?

My client, Zahra, feels broken when it comes to sex. It's hard for her to have an orgasm, and she's feeling discouraged and disconnected from Her Sexy. The more broken she feels, the more she wants to distance herself from her sexuality altogether. Together, we begin to look at the stories she has internalized about who and how she should be in the world.

When Zahra thinks about the women in her family, the words that come to her mind are: "busy, serving, and selfless." She thinks about her grandma preparing elaborate holiday meals while her grandpa watches television. She thinks about her mom working a full-time job and coming home to care for the house and everyone in it. Zahra also thinks about *herself*, and the myriad ways that the world has given her the message that she shouldn't take up too much space, she shouldn't make others feel uncomfortable, and she should be nice.

Zahra and I talk also about the ways in which she has been suppressing her various "appetites" forever. Zahra is careful about how much she eats, especially in social settings, for fear of being judged as too indulgent...too hungry. She is skilled at suppressing other appetites as well. She suppresses romantic interest, worrying about liking someone more than they like her...of seeming too hungry for love. As a relationship builds, she feels like she needs to suppress her sexual appetite as well for fear of seeming too hungry for sex.

Zahra's struggle with orgasm makes sense when we look, with radical compassion and total kindness, at these powerful stories she carries: Think of others before yourself and control your desires. Pleasure is, by its very nature, hungry, unruly, and selfish. Seeking pleasure begins with a sense that you are entitled to it. That you are worthy, by nature of your mere existence, of feeling good. Sexual pleasure is about *being* not *doing*, *receiving* not *giving*, *present-moment-focus* not *accomplishment*. No wonder so many women struggle to advocate for their own pleasure. The very nature of pleasure challenges and subverts much of what we are taught it is to be a woman.

As we unpack this, I want us to be careful not to conflate pleasure and orgasm. Unfortunately, we live in a world that perpetuates two particularly unhelpful stories about sexual pleasure: that *sexual pleasure equals orgasm* and that *orgasm equals successful sex*. We need to erase both stories ASAP.

- Pleasure does not equal orgasm. When we limit ourselves to a singular notion of what counts as pleasure, we miss the chance to create sexual experiences that meander curiously, leaving open possibilities for surprise, wonder, and connection.

- Orgasm does not equal successful sex. When we conflate pleasure and orgasm, there is just far too much pressure on ourselves to "perform." I feel clear that none of us is itching for yet another arena in which to figure out whether we are measuring up! Sex ought to be a space of respite from expectations to achieve.

Nothing will chase an orgasm away faster than a voice inside your head telling you that you need to have an orgasm. Well, nothing except a voice from a pressuring partner telling you that you need to have an orgasm.

Pressure and orgasm are enemies for sure. As sex therapist Stephen Snyder says, "in really good sex, orgasm should be like dessert at the end of a good meal. Memorable, perhaps. But not the reason you went out to dinner."[95] *While it is entirely possible to deeply and truly enjoy the pleasures of a sexual experience without having an orgasm, it is difficult to feel like you have permission to pursue an orgasm unless you feel entitled to pleasure.*

The Big O

Orgasm is yet another aspect of women's sexuality that has historically been poorly understood. In addition to being given the message that they weren't entitled to sexual pleasure, women have also been given the message that there are right and wrong ways for them to experience their orgasms. Back in the day, founding father of modern psychotherapy, Sigmund Freud, created a now-defunct theory that immature and neurotic women had orgasms from clitoral stimulation, while mature and healthy women had orgasms from vaginal stimulation.[96] In the 1970s, it was suggested that there were in fact three types of orgasms: vulval orgasms, uterine orgasms, and blended orgasms. (Don't worry about these names because they aren't even used anymore.) In the 1980s, people began to talk about G-spot orgasms—orgasms that result from stimulation of the front wall of the vagina.

So, where are we today? While labeling and cataloging orgasms may help women give language to their experiences, we must resist the urge to create a hierarchy of orgasms. Given what we now know about the expansive structure of the clitoris, it is likely that there is clitoral involvement in most if not all orgasms.[97] *Women's orgasms are diverse and dynamic.* An activity that resulted in an orgasm one day may not result in an orgasm on another day, and different sexual activities produce orgasms that feel different. For example, "some women describe G-spot orgasms as feeling more intense and 'wavelike' than clitoral orgasms, which are often described as powerful, sharp, or electric."[98]

If orgasms have been a source of stress in your life, it is not because you are broken but because you've been denied information that you are now claiming for yourself. As you authorize yourself to explore pleasure and orgasm, do so with mindfulness and self-compassion. Orgasms hate emotional pressure, so lead with curiosity and zero expectations.

In this larger context of silence, misinformation, and fear about women's sexual pleasure, it is wholly unsurprising that many studies have identified an orgasm gap between men and women. A study of six thousand men and women in the United States found a significant difference in orgasm frequency between men (85.1 percent) and women (62.9 percent). Here's where it gets especially interesting. For men, the mean orgasm rate did not vary by sexual orientation (gay men versus straight men versus bisexual men), but for women, the mean orgasm rate *varied significantly by sexual orientation.* Lesbian women (74.7 percent) had a significantly higher likelihood of orgasm than either heterosexual women (61.6 percent) or bisexual women (58 percent).[99]

Although life as a sexual minority is incredibly challenging on many fronts, these data suggest that when sexual experiences are created outside the old, narrow, and highly gendered sexual script, the potential for pleasure increases. When a man and a woman go to bed together, it is far too easy to fall prey to that rigid storyline. He is active; she is passive. He leads; she follows. He is entitled to pleasure; she is not. It's time to stop recreating the patriarchy in the bedroom. You deserve to feel entitled to the pursuit of an orgasm. When you wait for your partner to give you an orgasm, you are dimming your light. I invite you to take sexy back by writing a new story for yourself, one in which you are fully authorized to be an agent of your own plea-sure by bringing your orgasm to you.

If you're saying to yourself, "I don't know how to bring my orgasm to me," I have an answer that is simple but maybe not easy: masturba-tion. Masturbation is a powerful and effective way to get to know what feels good in your body. But cultural taboos against touching yourself are old and deep.[100] In 1994, President Bill Clinton fired Joycelyn Elders, the first African American person to serve as surgeon general of the United States, over backlash resulting from her comment that young people ought to be taught that masturbation is a "part of human sexuality." Some religious institutions consider "spilling your seed" to be sinful. Relegating masturbation to a taboo reinforces the idea that my body is not my own; it is solely for someone else's pleasure. While I have no interest in getting between you and your definitions of moral behavior, I cannot omit this powerful pathway to self-awareness. Female masturbation is associated with improvements in body image, self-awareness, and sexual pleasure, and it is sexually affirming and empowering.[101]

For Zahra, masturbation was a game changer. As she was begin-ning to challenge the gendered stories she was carrying about pleasure and selfishness, she started to date a woman who encouraged her to masturbate. In fact, one of their early dates involved a visit to a local sex shop where Zahra bought her first vibrator. She used it for the first time alone in her apartment and after she had an orgasm, she cried. As she explained, "It was so powerful to give myself the gift of that kind of pleasure. Rather than feeling selfish, I actually felt at home—worthy and deserving. It was like a new way of being inside of my body."

If masturbation feels new and scary, begin by thinking of masturbation in a broad and inclusive way. Masturbation is about bringing pleasure to yourself. Reflect on all of the ways that you currently bring pleasure to your body—twirling your hair, rubbing your leg, taking a hot bath, wrapping up in a cozy blanket. When you do these things, start to consciously associate them with the idea of self-pleasure. Consider the notion that masturbation is another point on a continuum of self-pleasure. If and when you feel ready to masturbate, remember that there is no right way or wrong way to do it. Except if something you're doing hurts, then don't do that! Try to take the pressure off yourself to have an orgasm. Instead, just try to learn what feels good to your body and what areas are wanting your attention. Find more support regarding masturbation in "Additional Resources for Your Sexy" at the back of the book.

It's never too late to get to know your body. Intimacy with your physicality and ease within your own skin set the stage for intimate connection with someone else.

＊

Your body is your sacred vessel. You've been living inside of it from day one, and it will carry you through all of your days. This body of yours deserves nothing short of your total reverence and love. It is the medium by which you get the chance to experience pleasure—touch, sight, smell, sound, and taste. Shedding shame-loaded judgments about your body and opting instead to be guided by self-compassion helps you cultivate an inside-out sense of Your Sexy. Your commitment to self-love offers healing and transformation to a world that has for too long asked women to be altruistic and pleasing.

emotional

Your Feelings Are Data

> I have lost count of how many women I've sat with, in the roots of their bodies, repairing the damage done by sexual abuse and violation. And let me be clear, the female body and energy system are far too powerful to be damaged by these acts—but what is damaged is the woman's connection to her own body, to her own knowing of her body as sacred. That connection between herself and her body is what must be repaired to heal.
>
> —Tami Lynn Kent, *Wild Feminine*

Emotion and sex have quite an intimate relationship! The arrow between sex and emotion goes in both directions. Our emotions can draw us toward sexual situations (or make us feel resistant or reluctant about sex). And sexual experiences stir emotions in us. This chapter will encourage you to make a commitment to honoring your emotions (the good, the bad, and the ugly) as the vital bits of data they are. We will talk about how to work with the feelings that sex stirs in you before, during, and after. We will then explore the impact of negative sexual experiences, including trauma, and the ever-present possibility of healing.

All the Feels

Experiencing and expressing emotions are central features of what it means to be a human being. Feelings act as indicator light from within, waking us up and asking us to pay attention. Emotions give color to our lives. They guide our choices, help us savor that which is sweet, and move us through that which is painful. Emotions are first and foremost *bodily states*—neurochemical and physiological processes. Thinking about our feelings and talking about our feelings are higher-order and subsequent processes. In other words, your emotions are raw data, and you then use thoughts and words to create meaning from your emotions.

Although we live in a culture that prizes independence and standing on our own two feet, we are profoundly relational creatures. Our best and bravest work is learning to lean into that paradox—I am *both* my own person *and* shaped by my relationships with others. Agency *and* communion. Grounded *and* connected. Given how relational we are, it is unsurprising that emotions are highly contagious. You know this in an intuitive and organic way. We've all had that experience of interacting with a friendly and upbeat cashier and then walking out of the store with a little more pep in our step. Or that experience of being in a good mood, hanging out with a friend who is a "Debbie Downer" and then walking away feeling like the world is a little grayer.

The more intimate the relationship, the more contagious the emotions. As researchers and clinicians Les Greenberg and Rhonda Goldman explain, "Partners affect each other's heart rate, breathing, perspiration, and physical well-being. When two people connect intimately, all kinds of neurochemical reactions occur. Unbeknownst to intimate partners, they produce little squirts of neurotransmitters in each other that send messages pouring through their partner's body. Affection is associated with pleasure, and the look or touch of a loved one sends endorphins on a complex journey through one's body. This is an especially pleasurable journey because endorphins are natural opiates that kill pain and produce pleasure. However, when people assert themselves or express hostility, testosterone, adrenaline, and cortisol all increase; muscles tense; and hearts beat faster."[102] There is no debating that relationships stir us emotionally. The only question is whether and how we will reckon with that reality.

Sexual Feelings

The arc of every sexual experience (the before, the during, the after) is imbued with emotion. The dangerous unhooking that occurs in hookup culture is not the unhooking of sex and commitment but rather the unhooking of sex and emotion. If we were mindfully attuned to our emotional state before, during, and after a sexual experience, I guarantee that we'd have something to say about the feelings associated with the experience. But there tends to be a troubling mindset in hookup culture that sex *ought not* stir up any emotions—a judgment that emotions equal drama. And I'm not even talking about falling-in-love emotions. I'm just talking about relating honestly to yourself about what your experiences stir in you. Because emotions are data, it is problematic to cut ourselves off from emotions that we have deemed to be messy, problematic, or weak. Disconnecting from emotions prevents us from asking for what we need and articulating healthy boundaries.

Begin a practice of connecting with your emotions before, during, and after your sexual experiences. Here's what you might notice:

> **Before.** The emotions we experience before sex are frequently tied up with sexual desire and driven by those core energies of love or fear. When *love* accompanies our transition into a sexual space with someone, it sounds like some version of this: "Let's have fun," "This is going to feel good," "I want to feel close to you." The emotions are longing, curiosity, love, and playfulness. When *fear* accompanies our transition into a sexual space with someone, it sounds like some version of this: "If we don't, you'll leave me or judge me," "I must do this to prove something," "I feel pressured to do this." The emotions are guilt, fear, and shame.

During. The emotions you experience during sex are hopefully those that indicate that you feel safe enough to open yourself, express yourself, and explore. When these are the emotions (happiness, excitement, gratitude), we feel less distracted and more mindful. If the emotions you experience are distressing, you need to be able to ask for a pause in order to figure out how to course-correct. Perhaps you can process the feeling and get back into the flow, but perhaps the feeling is too troubling, and you need to stop and snuggle, talk, or get some space.

After. Hopefully, the afterglow of a sexual experience is warm and happy. Cocreated casual sexual experiences yield feelings of ecstasy, empowerment, confidence, pride, and joy. Sexual experiences in the context of an intimate relationships can yield all of the above plus deepened empathy, trust, and commitment.

However, if sex sometimes leaves you feeling sad, you are not alone. In fact, since the days of the Roman Empire, people have noted post-coital dysphoria (PCD), feeling blue after sex, briefly or up to a couple days. About half of women (46 percent) report having experienced PCD.[103] Researchers have also found that nearly half of men (41 percent) have experienced PCD in their lifetime and 20 percent reported experiencing PCD in the previous four weeks.[104] These researchers found that PCD was somewhat more likely to occur in people who are experiencing current psychological distress, people who experienced childhood sexual abuse, and people who are struggling with a sexual dysfunction. That sense of sadness might be readily tied to the context of the sexual experience—you felt pressured into having sex, your partner was unkind or not attuned to you, your partner was cold after sex when you craved connection, or you were bothered by negatively-charged thoughts or feelings during sex. But that sadness might also feel more inexplicable. Some professionals believe that PCD is a quirk in some people's neurochemistry.[105] Other professionals have wondered if PCD happens because sex puts us face-to-face with life's deepest truths. As a powerful means of communion and connection, sex allows us, for the moment at least, to escape that knowledge that each of us ultimately comes into this world alone and leaves it alone too.

Rather than taking you down an existential rabbit hole, I am bringing PCD to your attention as a reminder of two things. Sex and emotion are inextricably bound. And, sexual self-awareness is about staying connected to what stirs in you before, during, and after a sexual experience. Remember: emotions are the data; thoughts create the meaning. If you experience PCD, be careful of the meaning you make about your feelings. Perhaps your feelings of sadness after sex are inviting you to check in with yourself about the motivation that led you into the experience in the first place. Perhaps these feelings are letting you know that something is amiss in this relationship and needs your attention. Perhaps your feelings simply speak to that vague ache of being human, and the antidote is to snuggle closer to your partner and let the tears flow.

Write responsively to the following questions about your last several sexual experiences:

- What were you feeling before you entered a sexual space with your partner?

- What were you feeling during the sexual experience?

- What were you feeling after?

See if you can make a distinction between the emotions themselves and the meaning you made about the emotions.

In the previous exercise, I asked you to practice discerning the emotions themselves from the meaning you make of the emotions. Because we are meaning-making creatures, we often make meaning so quickly that we "lose" the raw data of the emotions. It's helpful to practice distinguishing between the emotions and the meaning because it allows you to inhabit a space of greater possibility and choice.

Stephanie and Toby have been together for eight years. Stephanie experiences a lot of anxiety in her sexual relationship with Toby. When they have sex, she feels a tremendous sense of relief. If she tries to initiate sex and he declines because he's tired, she feels scared. When she feels they are sexually disconnected, she worries. The meaning she makes of all this fear is that he doesn't love her anymore and he's going to leave her for another partner. In addition to her internal suffering, this emotion-meaning spiral of feeling afraid and becoming convinced that he's going to leave also creates relational fallout. The more anxious and insecure Stephanie gets, the more Toby feels smothered and consequently withdraws.

As Stephanie began to address the ways in which she relies on sex to regulate her emotional world, she could see how quickly she moves from emotion (anxiety) to meaning (he's going to leave me; we aren't okay). This awareness allowed her to name the anxiety—to herself and to Toby. "When you don't want to make love, I get scared that we are doomed." Toby responded, "It feels like a lot of pressure to me, that I only have one way of making you feel cared for. If you're feeling scared and I'm not really available for sex, how else could I let you know that I'm here and I care about you?" This new conversation soothed Stephanie's soul, helping her tap into other possibilities for the connection and reassurance she previously felt could only come through sex.

Now, we need to address some of the more difficult emotions that Your Sexy may be experiencing.

Sexual Alarm System

Attending to the "dark" helps us savor and enhance the "light." As Brené Brown explains, "We cannot selectively numb emotions, when we numb the painful emotions, we also numb the positive emotions."[106] Painful emotions that your sexual self carries deserve your most self-compassionate care and attention. By facing what hurts, we can reach for that which holds the power to heal.

Sex cannot be separated from vulnerability. Getting naked with another person, even in a casual sexual encounter, involves vulnerability and risk. Inadequate sex education and a lack of conversation about sexuality in our homes as we are growing up sow seeds of sexual shame that amplify vulnerability. And there's something else—an emotional tax that is levied on us simply as a result of growing up female. Sexual violence against women is endemic in our culture—35 percent of heterosexual women, 44 percent of lesbian women, and 61 percent of bisexual women carry the trauma of sexual violence.[107] But 100 percent of us have experienced the *little-t trauma*, which is living with the pervasive fear of sexual violence.

A brief word on big-T and little-t trauma. In an effort to make space for a fuller range of experiences that can leave behind painful knots of emotion that we associate with trauma—hypervigilance, shame, fear, and difficulties with trust—people in the mental health field have begun to talk not only about what is traditionally considered a trauma (big-T trauma) but also about little-t trauma. The line between these two kinds of trauma is fuzzy, but what distinguishes a big-T trauma is the fear of loss of life or loss of bodily integrity. Examples of little-t traumas include rejection from your family in the coming-out process, a painful breakup or divorce, infidelity, invisibility or unfair treatment resulting from systemic racism, or losing a loved one. Both big-T traumas and little-t traumas shape who we are and how we relate to other people.

Coming into your sexuality in a culture that teaches boys and men that they are predators and girls and women that they are prey is itself a little-t trauma. To be female is to have grown up with a very real and legitimate fear of being sexually assaulted. Women learn to be vigilant to potential danger. And women are taught that *any* unwanted attention (from catcalls to sexual assault) is their fault. One of my students recalls being told as a teenager that she was dressed too sexy and thinking to herself, *Too sexy for what?*

Activist Jackson Katz is passionate about illuminating the ways in which our culture condones and perpetuates violence against women. He says, "We talk about how many women were raped last year, not about how many men raped women. We talk about how many girls in a school district were harassed last year, not about how many boys harassed girls. We talk about how many teenage girls in the state of

Vermont got pregnant last year, rather than how many men and boys impregnated teenage girls. So you can see how the use of the passive voice has a political effect. [It] shifts the focus off of men and boys and onto girls and women. Even the term 'violence against women' is problematic. It's a passive construction; there's no active agent in the sentence. It's a bad thing that happens to women, but when you look at that term 'violence against women,' nobody is doing it to them. It just happens to them... Men aren't even part of it!"[108]

The thing about little-t traumas is that they accumulate, with emotions and adaptations building up slowly over time. Therapist Judith Leavitt uses the term "the sexual alarm system" to describe the adaptations that women make as a result of living in a culture replete with violence against women.[109] By dint of their female bodies, women are wired to be alert to danger, making it difficult to respond to touch with openness and excitement—even when that touch is wanted. The process may be subtle. Her partner comes up behind her in the kitchen and grabs her butt. Although her rational brain knows she is safe, her emotional brain may code danger, leading her body to shift, tensing up and pulling away. If she then immediately overrides her sexual alarm system so she can go on to have sex with her partner, she reinforces the link between sex and danger.

Leavitt encourages women to learn to recognize situations that trigger their sexual alarm system and to communicate those triggers to their partner. It is also helpful for women to tune in to their body so they can find ways to enter into sexual experiences without tripping the alarm. In the kitchen example above, where her alarm had already been tripped, she would benefit from just taking a moment to ground herself in her body using a mindfulness tool. That way, she shuts off her alarm and ensures that she's fully present and safe in her body before she connects with her partner sexually. It is difficult and courageous to do two seemingly opposite things at once in this world—feel enraged that sexual violence persists *and* do what it takes to enjoy your sexuality nonetheless.

Trauma and Recovery

Let's turn our attention now to big-T trauma. One-time traumas include surviving a terrible incident like a crime (being sexually assaulted, robbed, or otherwise attacked) or a natural disaster (tornado, hurricane, or flood). Enduring traumas involve an ongoing relationship and include surviving something like domestic violence, neglect, kidnapping, bullying, or emotional, physical, or sexual abuse.

Traumatic events can leave a variety of scars. Initially following the event, people may suffer from feelings of shock or denial. Over the long term, people may experience unpredictable emotions, flashbacks, relationship problems, and physical symptoms like headaches or nausea. These are signs of post-traumatic stress disorder (PTSD). When traumas endure over many months or years—like growing up in an abusive home or being in an abusive intimate relationship—they can result in symptoms like relationship problems, physical problems, difficulty regulating emotions, dissociation or losing time, struggles with impulse control, cognitive issues (attention problems, executive functioning problems), and lack of self-esteem or poor self-concept. Therapists sometimes refer to symptoms like these as "complex trauma."

The field of trauma studies is amazing, and clinicians and researchers have powerful tools for healing the wounds created by trauma. If you are a survivor of trauma, I encourage you to connect with a mental health professional who can support your healing journey. "Additional Resources for Your Sexy" has suggestions to help you get started.

If you are someone who has yet to seek help in the recovery process, what is keeping you from starting therapy? Sometimes geographic or financial constraints are to blame. But sometimes the nature of trauma prevents recovery. Nearly every trauma survivor carries some version of self-recrimination, a sense that they are to blame for their trauma. Sometimes the perpetrator tells them what happened was their fault. Sometimes people in the survivor's life convey that they should have known better, should have stopped it, shouldn't have been there in the first place. The part of you that has internalized that story may struggle to feel authorized to claim time and space to recover. *That part of you deserves to know that she is innately, profoundly, and fully worthy of feeling whole again.*

What did the quote that opens this chapter stir in you? When I first read it, I felt like I was being punched in the gut. Sexual violence against women is the most wretched form of desecrating, punishing, and silencing the feminine. The author of this quote, Tami Kent, is a physical therapist who has developed an integrative approach to working with women's pelvic bowls (hips and genitals) to help them recover from injuries and traumas that range from hysterectomies to sexual trauma. The optimism of Kent's words gets me every time. A woman who has been sexually traumatized is far from broken. What has been broken is the connection between herself and her body. Healing is about helping her come back home to herself. Healing is a process of reclamation. Healing from trauma is scary and difficult and beautiful. And more than anything, healing from trauma is possible. As Ralph Waldo Emerson said, "What lies behind us and what lies before us are tiny matters compared to what lies within us."

Intimate Partner as Ally

People who suffer big-T trauma sometimes cope with the pain by pushing away memories and feelings about the trauma, determined that nobody has to know and wanting desperately to believe that the trauma has no impact on them today. As trauma expert Bessel van der Kolk explains, "As long as you keep secrets and suppress information, you are fundamentally at war with yourself...the critical issue is allowing yourself to know what you know. That takes an enormous amount of courage."[110] Even if you *think* that your traumatic memories are adequately stuffed away, pain, left unattended, persists. Inevitably, something happens that awakens the past. *Often that something is building an intimate, emotional, and sexual relationship with someone.*

Trauma (especially complex trauma) involves a breach of trust in an important relationship, and trauma teaches you to live on high alert, prepared to fend off the next danger. But intimate relationships and sexual experiences require us to open ourselves up, to trust, to let our guard down. Building a romantic relationship with someone is, by its very nature, *retraumatizing*, and the intimate relationship may at times evoke feelings that are similar to feelings you had in the context of the abusive relationship. Sex can be especially triggering. Even with a trustworthy and loving intimate partner, survivors of trauma can experience flashbacks or intrusive thoughts (uninvited thoughts that pop into your head) related to the trauma. Working with a therapist who specializes in trauma can help. Sexual trauma is, by definition, relational, and the healing process is as well.

A healthy intimate relationship can be an incredibly healing force in the life of someone who has lived through trauma. I have been moved to tears many times in therapy when a client takes the risk of bravely sharing with their intimate partner a painful memory from the past. In that moment, courage claims victory over shame. And there is no more powerful healer of shame than connection. But self-work and self-care are the sturdiest foundations of your healing. Love alone is not enough.

Healing is a "within and between" process. My client, Maria, was sexually assaulted five years ago. She has been on a healing journey *within*—availing herself of a variety of therapeutic tools to help her reclaim what trauma took from her. Also her intimate relationship with a boyfriend of two years, Charles, has become a crucible for further healing—a healing journey *between* the two of them.

Traumatic events create a disorder of memory. Trauma has no time stamp, so it's common for survivors to confuse the past and the present. When that happens, it's so helpful to be near someone you trust. One night, Maria and Charles were playing a heated game of Scrabble. When Maria beat him handily, Charles crawled over to her side of the couch to make her "pay" for her victory, snuggling her hard and covering her in kisses. Maria was laughing, but something about the position of their bodies ended up triggering her. She yelled, "Stop!"

but the brief space between her yell and his release felt like an eternity. Her heart was racing, she felt terrified, and she began to cry.

Because Maria and Charles had talked about what being an intimate ally looked like, Charles knew what to do in that moment. He stopped touching her and scooted away from her. He spoke softly and in short sentences: "I'm here. It's me. You're safe." Maria was able to lock into his rhythmic voice, which calmed her, and his gentle eyes oriented her. By giving her space, he reminded her that she has bodily autonomy. By refocusing her, he helped her find the path from past to present. Maria watched the rise and fall of his chest, and she matched her breathing to his. She felt her panic subside, and she was soon able to lean into him, crying tears of relief, not terror.

Maria has been in the process of taking Her Sexy back for years by compassionately and gently learning how to honor the data from her body. Although her journey of reclamation has been and remains her own, she now has a fellow traveler—Charles. She uses her relational and sexual self-awareness to advocate for what she needs to feel safe and connected in this relationship. He uses his relational and sexual self-awareness to learn what it means to be her ally. Central to being an ally is a commitment not to get defensive in the face of a trauma survivor's flooding. Imagine how much differently this would have gone if Charles had rolled his eyes and said, "Come on, Maria! It's just me! I can't believe something as simple as tickling can trigger you!" We all need and deserve trusting relationships, ones that allow us to be both brave and tender. It is essential for survivors of trauma to advocate for themselves in ways that honor their vulnerabilities *and* to choose intimate partners who can hear, understand, and respect the courage it takes to trust again.

If you are working to reclaim Your Sexy in the aftermath of a sexual trauma, here are a few concluding reminders:

Slow and steady. Make a commitment that you will not continue to be sexual if you get triggered. Take a break, come back into your body, and then decide whether and how you want to proceed sexually.

Expect setbacks. Healing is not a linear process. You will likely take two steps forward and one step back. Don't give up.

Ask for help. From a therapist, from other survivors, and from your partner.

Believe in yourself. Trust your resilience and your ability to heal, grow, and reclaim Your Sexy.

Recovering from trauma is hard work, work that survivors need and deserve so they can live more comfortably in their own skin. Reclaiming Your Sexy after trauma is also a way of saying to the perpetrator(s): "You hurt me, but you did not break me."

Emotions are bodily cues. Cues that lead us to act—pull back, reach out, cry, laugh. Energy medicine expert Donna Eden says, "When I smile, it doesn't actually feel like I am smiling. It feels more like an energy is smiling me. I love to feel that energy come up through my face, my cheeks, my eyes, and permeate my entire being."[111] Honoring the inextricable bond between emotion and sex opens new possibilities for Your Sexy.

❁

You are, by design, an emotional creature. Taking sexy back means that, rather than denying or deflecting, you instead lean fully and unapologetically into that truth because you know your emotions are a trustworthy compass. Your Sexy needs you to tune in to the rich data that live in your body and advocate for connection from that place of wisdom and awareness. This is the brave and tender work of a lifetime.

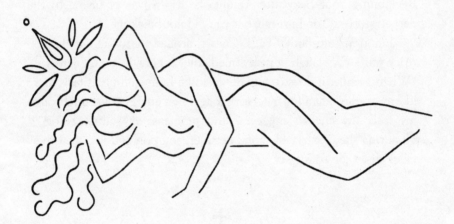

relational

The Space Between You and Your Partner

I was always ashamed to take. So I gave. It was not a virtue. It was a disguise.

—Anais Nin, *The Diary of Anais Nin, Vol. 4*

A long time ago, in a galaxy far, far away, my now-husband, Todd, and I were dating. We were hanging out in his apartment, and it became clear to me that it was time to transition from hanging out to, you know, hanging out. And I got this idea in my head that a great way to get this party started would be to perform...*a naked handstand*. He was (surprise, surprise) more than happy to watch. So, I slid over to the jam box (we were pre-Spotify in this story) and turned on Joe Cocker's "You Can Leave Your Hat On," which was, and remains, the greatest seduction song of all time. I broke out all my sweet dance moves as I disrobed. You must know that at this moment in the story, I am positively filled to the brim with divine sexual goddess energy, right? All eyes are on me. I own this space. I've got him right where I want him. I shimmy on over to the wall and kick up into my handstand. On the way up, I whack my foot against the back of his couch and go flying head first into the wall, landing in a pile of nakedness and despair.

I can tell you this story and worry only a little about you judging me because of how the memory is encoded in my brain. It's a story full of sweetness and humor for me, and that is largely because of how Todd responded. He raced over and covered me with his body. He held me, and we laughed.

Although you may very well be scarred for life by hearing about my tragic seduction, the story gets us focused on the *between* aspect of sex. Remember in chapter 6 when we talked about how sex is both within and between, requiring us to be both *grounded* within ourselves and *connected* to our partner? It's time for us to dig into the space between you and your partner by exploring the relational aspects of Your Sexy. In this chapter, we will explore what it takes to have happy sex with the same person again and again and how to talk with your partner about sex.[112]

An intimate relationship is alive. It grows and changes over time. The psychology and physiology of initial attraction and interest are *different from* the psychology and physiology of ongoing connection and commitment. A couple's sex life is messy and imperfect, requiring of both partners hearty doses of curiosity, patience, effort, empathy, and humor. In your life together as a couple, you will continue to crave *both* novelty *and* security, *both* risk *and* safety, *both* surprise *and* comfort. You are invited and challenged to make space for both.

Sex Matters

The quality of a couple's sex life matters. Feeling sexually satisfied is strongly positively correlated with mental health, physical health, and relationship satisfaction for mixed-sex and same-sex couples.[113] These variables live in a feedback loop: when couples feel good about their sexual connection, they feel better individually and collectively, and when people feel better individually and collectively, they can invest with joy in their sexual connection. Sex therapist Barry McCarthy found that feeling sexually satisfied adds about 15 to 20 percent to a couple's marital vitality and satisfaction. "When sexuality is conflictual, dysfunctional, or nonexistent, it plays an inordinately powerful role, 50 to 70 percent, in draining the marriage of intimacy and vitality."[114] Great sex certainly cannot make a bad relationship into a good one, but it can make a good relationship better. And it can keep a good relationship strong.

Desire Discrepancy Is a Couple Challenge

Couples often find that sexual desire was quite robust in the early stages of their intimate relationship but that it fades over time.[115] Just knowing that it is normal for sexual desire to ebb and flow in an intimate relationship can go a long way toward helping couples shift their perspective. Couples must ask themselves: "To what degree are we thinking that something is wrong with me, you, or us instead of understanding that changes in sexual desire are normal and expected?"

In sharing her relationship history, a new client of mine shared that she had just broken up with her boyfriend. She said, "In the beginning, our sex life was great, but after a while, we stopped having it as frequently. I just believe that when the sex goes bad, the relationship goes bad, so that was a big part of our breakup." She took the *fact* of decreasing sexual frequency and attached to it a fear-based *story*: this must mean we are not right for each other. Her story makes total sense in a culture that runs on romanticized notions that if love requires effort, it means you're doing it wrong. I wonder what might have been different for them if someone had whispered in her ear that sexual desire shifts with familiarity and commitment and that couples need to work together to cultivate desire over time.

Sexual desire problems are often *desire discrepancy problems*—one partner wants to have sex more often than the other. The chances of two partners always experiencing the exact same levels of sexual desire are slim to none, but any point of relational difference holds the potential to become a point of relational tension and pain. In the face of desire discrepancy, it tends to be easy to stick a "high-desire partner" label on one member of the couple and a "low-desire partner" label on the other. As with any label, we must proceed with caution. A label can normalize and validate something that feels upsetting or confusing. But a label can also make something complicated appear deceptively simple. Declaring, "I am the high-desire partner, and you are the low-desire partner" can put a couple at risk of slipping into stories full of shame and blame:

- If you loved me, you'd want more sex.

- If you loved me, you'd stop expecting so much sex.

- You're frigid/repressed/depressed.

- You're a sex addict.

- I must be frigid/repressed/depressed.

- I must be a sex addict.

Shame- and blame-loaded stories only know how to do two things: make me right and you wrong or make you right and me wrong. They are boring dead ends! And these narrow stories create relational loops that tend to amplify: the more I tell you that you should want more sex, the more you're going to pull away, and the more you pull away, the more I'm going to persist. Couples therapists call this a "pursuer-withdrawer dynamic."

We break the cycle by remembering both partners need and deserve compassion. Being the one who initiates intimacy again and again can stir feelings of loneliness, rejection, and inadequacy. Being the sexual gatekeeper, declining or avoiding your partner's advances, can stir feelings of resentment and shame because it's hard to disappoint the people we love.

We also break the cycle by remembering that *all sexual problems are couple problems*. Use the Golden Equation of Love (my stuff + your stuff = our stuff) to keep the desire discrepancy framed as a *we* issue. Stand shoulder to shoulder, looking together at the problem. Ask yourselves and each other this question: "What are *we* going to do to nurture sexual intimacy in this relationship?"

Sexual intimacy stirs our internal worlds deeply—our old stories, our wounds, our longings, and our needs. With that kind of complexity, it's wholly unsurprising that most couples encounter a sexual challenge of one kind or another. The shift from a shame-loaded or blame-loaded story to a story that holds compassion for yourself and your partner opens new possibilities for how to address the problem.

Your Sexy's Sacred Trio: Risk, Self-Compassion, and Trust

I want to introduce you to something I call Your Sexy's Sacred Trio: risk, self-compassion, and trust.

Your Sexy's Sacred Trio

Sex involves at least some amount of *risk*, the first element of the Sacred Trio. We can mitigate physical risks like STIs and unplanned pregnancy by taking precautions that protect us, and that is obviously foundational and mandatory. But the emotional and relational risks that come with sexual expression are a bit trickier. Any relational step we take—telling someone we like them, committing to a relationship, getting naked for the first time, letting your partner know you want to have sex tonight, sharing a sexual fantasy, indulging a partner's sexual fantasy—involves at least some amount of risk because the other person's response is never guaranteed. We can't override the tension that inevitably arises when we put ourselves out there, asserting ourselves by declaring what we want or need. Nor would we want to because the moment we numb ourselves in order to block the fear of embarrassment, we also numb ourselves to the stuff we actually want to feel like pride, joy, and closeness because there is no such thing as selective numbing.

The goal isn't to eliminate risk in order to ensure total emotional safety. In addition to being impossible, it's undesirable. With level-zero risk, a sexual experience leaves the River of Integration and ends up washed ashore the boring bank of rigidity. Some amount of risk is energizing and enlivening, bringing us to full attention and presence. Practicing sexual self-awareness is about figuring out, for you and for now, how to titrate risk and safety so Your Sexy can express herself.

Sex always brings with it the possibility of the absurd, the inane, the embarrassing. The images we consume of other people's sexual experiences, from romantic comedies to pornography, don't show this to us. But in real life sex, stuff goes wrong. The dog starts scratching on the door. Erections get lost. Somebody gets a foot cramp. Make sure that you think critically about the images of sex you consume and remind yourself often of the conspicuous gap between movie sex and real-life sex. Talk with your partner about how to embrace together the profoundly imperfect nature of sex. Name it to tame it.[116] Shame has the tendency to dissolve in the light of day, so acknowledging out loud to each other that real-life sex is quirky and imperfect goes a long way toward turning down the pressure and turning up the play.

My handstand was a *risk*—a moment in which I allowed My Sexy to express something that felt authentic. Whenever we take a risk, we must accept that in the space between idea and execution, stuff may go awry. Though profoundly flawed, look what it opened up. It gave Todd an opportunity to step into a deeply empathic space. Instead of retreating in disgust or laughing at me, he met me in a vulnerable place—physically and emotionally. In doing so, he got to experience that yummy blend of pride and closeness that comes when you attune yourself deeply to the experience of another. And I got to experience the deep exhale that comes when you get to be imperfect and loved anyway!

Here's the catch though. When Todd approached me, in order for me to receive his empathy, I needed at least a modicum of *self-compassion*, the second element of Your Sexy's Sacred Trio. Without self-compassion, the whole situation would have felt really threatening to me. And, mammals that we are, when threatened, we go into fight-or-flight mode. Here's what responding from a space of fight or flight would have looked like:

Fight. I would have found a way to attack or blame him, making this whole thing into his fault. It sounds totally illogical, but when shame meets up with a lack of self-compassion, we end up with some seriously sketchy, knee-jerk responses.

Flight. I would have retreated—literally, by running into the bathroom, or figuratively by getting quiet and closed off. Shame pulls us out of connection because shame says, "I am unlovable and unworthy of comfort."

With self-compassion though, we can hang in there during those tender moments. We need and deserve self-compassion in all facets of our lives, but given the emotional riskiness of sex, we desperately need to relate to Our Sexy with fierce self-compassion. Self-compassion helps you say, "I've got you, Sexy! Take the risk of expressing yourself because you are worthy no matter what."

Self-compassion helps you be brave enough to try, while letting go of the outcome (which cannot be known…that's why it's a risk). But the power of self-compassion gets supercharged when you cocreate with a trustworthy intimate partner. The third element of Your Sexy's Sacred Trio, *trust*, allows you to say, "Sexy, this relational space can handle you. This partner has earned the right to see you in all your glory. You can take a risk, and they will love you regardless of the outcome." Ensure that the Sacred Trio of risk, self-compassion, and trust accompanies you into the bedroom.

Let's look at another example of this trio in action. Tori has been with her boyfriend, Trey, for about eighteen months, and the safety she feels with him allows her to expand the boundaries of her sexual curiosity. One night they were fooling around, and Tori took the risk of expressing a fantasy of hers. "Trey," Tori said. "I want you to come on my face and call me a whore." Trey obliged. When they were done, Tori felt a rush of shame and sadness. In that awful moment, the trust that allowed her to take the risk of bringing a sexual fantasy to life with Trey was the very same trust that allowed her to turn toward him with her distress. "That felt awful to me," Tori cried. Trey stayed present, holding her as the emotions washed over her. After a while, Tori began to feel a little distance from the experience. "Well," she joked, "apparently not all fantasies are so awesome in real life!" An experience like this could have lingered, leaving behind a residue of regret and ick. It didn't because, after taking that risk, Tori practiced self-compassion, reminding herself that her sexual desires remain worthy of exploration, and she leaned into the relational trust that she and Trey had built together.

Erotic Imagination

Todd and I were reminiscing about the ill-fated handstand recently, and he remembered agreeing to witness the handstand but that the whole premise wasn't particularly titillating to him. The handstand was about *me turning myself on*, owning my wanting and playing with a fantasy about my desirability. He was the supporting actor to my starring role. Researchers call this "object of desire self-consciousness"— the perception that one is romantically or sexually desirable in another person's eyes.[117] Object of desire self-consciousness is a feedback loop that goes like this: watching you be turned on by me turns me on. There is a gender difference, as women are more likely than men to fantasize about being the object of another person's desire.[118] Women's sexual desire is perhaps more narcissistic and less relational than we've been led to believe.[119]

Object of desire self-consciousness is just one of an infinite number of sexual fantasies available to Your Sexy. Sexual fantasies are defined as conscious thoughts and mental images that generate sexual arousal. Sex researcher Dr. Justin Lehmiller conducted the largest-ever study of Americans' sexual fantasies, gathering data from over four thousand men and women, and his research makes clear that sexual fantasies are normal. The vast majority of us (97 percent) have them.[120] *Exploring your relationship with your erotic imagination grows your sexual self-awareness.* If you are someone who has sexual fantasies, what is your relationship with those fantasies? Perhaps you have historically judged your fantasy world, thinking that the existence of these naughty images meant that you were dirty or perverted. What might be different for you if you related to your sexual fantasies as both normal and yours?

Are you curious to know what people are fantasizing about? In analyzing the data, Lehmiller was able to classify most fantasies into one of seven broad themes.[121] Here they are, listed here in order of popularity:

1. Multipartner sex, like threesomes and orgies

2. Power, control, and rough sex

3. Novelty, adventure, and variety, like never-attempted sex acts, unique settings, like a beach or an airplane, or thrilling encounters, like having sex in public

4. Taboo and forbidden sex, including fetishes like licking someone's feet, watching people having sex, or having people watch you have sex

5. Partner-sharing and nonmonogamous relationships

6. Passion and romance—fantasies about intense sexual attraction, intimacy, belonging, and connection

7. Erotic flexibility, specifically, homoeroticism and gender-bending—fantasies about cross-dressing, being with a partner who is cross-dressing, or imagining sex that is inconsistent with your actual sexual orientation, like straight sex if you are a lesbian woman

What stood out most to Lehmiller was that in our fantasy life, many of us crave an opportunity to break free from cultural norms and sexual restraints. Normalizing sexual fantasies goes a long way toward freeing us from shame. As Lehmiller says, "The more shame, embarrassment, and anxiety people feel about their sexual desires, the more likely they are to avoid talking about sex at all and to experience sexual performance difficulties, finding it challenging to become (or stay) aroused or to reach orgasm."[122] I invite you to let go of any judgment you may be carrying about your sexual fantasies. They are yours and yours alone—offering a space you can go to heal, explore, and escape. Especially if you are someone who primarily experiences responsive desire, give yourself permission to use your sexual fantasies to spark sexual desire. Let yourself have naughty thoughts, and your body will follow.

Your sexual fantasies are an erotic blueprint of sorts.[123] Relate to your sexual fantasies as stories that can be mined for themes that reflect your pain points and yearnings—for control, for surrender, for invisibility, for attention. For example, someone who had to overfunction in their family as they were growing up because they had parents who were addicted or depressed or otherwise unavailable may have a sexual fantasy about being lavished with sexual attention. Someone who was bullied and marginalized as a kid growing up may have a sexual fantasy in which they are dominant and powerful. A sexual fantasy may be an attempt to heal, to understand, or to master something that has been a source of pain. Relating to your fantasies as avenues of self-discovery will help you shift from judgment to curiosity and help you appreciate the deep wisdom of Your Sexy.

Although you are also fully entitled to keep your sexual fantasies right between your ears as your private playground, you may well want your fantasy to come to life. Lehmiller found that most of the people he surveyed reported that they *do* want to act out their favorite fantasy (79 percent). Of those who acted out their fantasies in real life, most reported that the lived experience of the fantasy met or exceeded their expectations (86 percent) and that it had a neutral to positive effect on their relationship (91 percent).[124]

Exploring sexual fantasies is one way that couples keep their sexual spark alive, but other stuff is helpful too. Research with a sample of almost forty thousand heterosexual men and women in long-term intimate relationships looked at sexually happy couples' secrets to success. LGBTQ+ readers, I see you, and your stories need to be included in research! In this sample, about half of the people reported being satisfied with their current sex lives, and about one in three participants (38 percent of women; 32 percent of men) claimed their sex lives were as passionate now as in the beginning of the relationship. Sexual satisfaction and passion were higher among those who had sex most frequently, who received more oral sex, who had more consistent orgasms, and who incorporated more variety of sexual acts, mood, setting, and sexual communication.[125] So let's talk next about talking about sex.

> Write an erotic short story. Before you begin, take some deep breaths and open yourself to creativity and possibility. Let go of judgment and expectation. Create your characters, set the scene, and describe the action. Notice what's happening inside of you as you write. Are you feeling turned on and able to enjoy your arousal? After you've written the story, try to look at the story from some distance. What do the themes in the story suggest about what you yearn for? What do the themes suggest that you're needing to master or understand?

Giving Your Sexy Voice: Sexual Communication

The self-awareness journey you're taking in this book will make it easier to advocate on behalf of Your Sexy. One of the members of my graduate team shared with me that in the process of working on this book, she was having a lot of fun getting to know Her Sexy—letting go of shame-loaded stories that felt limiting and cultivating a deep love for the power and beauty of her body. Her private and sacred inner work changed the space between her and her partner. She described that although she had been enjoying their sex life, she was becoming curious about what else might be possible as she began to live in her body in a more empowered and self-compassionate way. Given that her partner is male (and therefore socialized to believe that he always needs to be in charge), she worried that he would hear her desire to explore and play as a criticism that he wasn't satisfying her. Nevertheless, she took the risk of talking with him about some of her insights and desires, and she was delighted that he expressed excitement about going on this journey with her. Is there a more beautiful way to imagine a couple's sex life? An unfolding journey of exploration and play.

Unfortunately, a lot of couples don't feel able to have these conversations. Researchers have found that in relationships that were over a decade old, partners understood only about 60 percent of what their partner liked sexually and only around 20 percent of what they didn't like sexually.[126] And being able to talk with each other about sex is tied to all kinds of good stuff like sexual desire, sexual arousal, lubrication, orgasm, erectile function, and less pain.[127] Talking with a partner about sex grows trust, *and* building trust makes it easier to talk about sex. Relationship scientist Dr. Sue Johnson says, "In fact, surveys tell us that in real life, folks in long-term relationships who can talk openly about their sex life have more and better sex than new or more reticent couples. What really determines what kind of sex you are going to have isn't the novel positions you find in the sex manual or the new tips in the latest magazine. It's how safely attached you are to your partner. Emotional presence and trust are the biggest aphrodisiacs of all."[128]

Talking about sex may come naturally for you. Or maybe the mere thought of figuring out and asking for what you want in bed brings a flush to your cheeks. If you are a card-carrying member of Team Blushy Face, no worries. I've got you covered! The good news is that you don't need to talk like a porn star (unless you want to) to get Your Sexy what she wants and needs. Start by completing this sentence: *It is difficult for me to talk to my partner about sex because* _____.

Where does your response fit within the Map of Sexual Self-Awareness? Is it a gendered message about what "nice girls" do and don't do? Is it an emotion like shame that gets in the way? Perhaps you are still settling into the notion of sexual self-advocacy.

A common response is: "I'm afraid of hurting my partner's feelings." If the fear of seeming cruel resonates for you, let me first say that this makes total sense. Sex makes us feel vulnerable, so your empathy for your partner shows your sensitivity. An intimate relationship is not a communication free-for-all, and we certainly need to be considerate and mindful about how we raise concerns. In addition, if your partner is someone who has been acculturated in the masculine, there's a sneaky gender script at work here too. You may be aware that he carries a story that goes like this: "As a man, *I* am responsible for my partner's pleasure. If she doesn't think the sex is mind-blowing, it's *my* fault." That incredibly unhelpful story is part of why I included chapter 12 in this book. As you reclaim Your Sexy and take responsibility for self-advocacy, you take some pressure off your partner, especially if your partner is male. But your work needs to go hand in hand with *his* work of no longer equating your orgasm and his manliness. That old gendered script is exhausting for you both!

Regardless of how you completed the above sentence stem, here are some suggestions that can help you give voice to Your Sexy:

Be positive. Frame your conversations about sex in the most positive light possible—you want to talk about sex in order to enhance what you already have. As sex therapist Dr. Tammy Nelson says, "Instead of saying, 'don't go left,' say, 'I love it when you go right!'"[129]

Talk outside of the bedroom. Some people find it better and easier to talk about sex during a nonsexual time rather than in the heat of the moment. Be on the lookout for conversation-starters. Talking about a sexy scene from a movie can segue into talking about the two of you. I also hope this book will be a conversation-starter.

Think outside the box. I'm all for face-to-face conversation, but it's certainly not the only way. Communication can happen on all kinds of different "channels." Over the past few years, I've been collecting a list of creative ways to talk about hard stuff with your partner. Some of these ideas come from research and articles, and some of these ideas come from couples I have been fortunate to get to know though my work.

- *Use an app.* Kindu is a swipe-based app that you and your partner put on your phones. The app gives you a list of possible sexual experiences from positions to fantasies to settings. Each of you swipes left on the items that you're not up for and right on the items you find intriguing, and the app gives you a customized menu of shared possibilities.

- *Set the scene.* One couple I know saves all their difficult dialogs for the bathtub because the warm water and relaxed vibe open them more deeply to each other. Maybe for the two of you it's in a tent, in the car, on a hike. Identify the settings that open you to each other and the ones that shut you down.

- *Write letters.* We live in an era of immediate digital communication, but sex demands a slow and full-sensory vibe. Writing letters to each other can be both intimacy-promoting and seductive. If you prefer a modern twist, Esther Perel encourages couples to create email accounts that they will use *only* for conversations about love and sex.[130] No logistics allowed.

- *Use puppets.* Talking about sex through a puppet (or another character) may allow Your Sexy to say some things that your everyday self would censor. When a couple shared this secret to success with me, I was smiling ear to ear. When we enter the realm of the erotic, we are transported, altered, different from our ordinary selves.

- *Try an accent.* After I gave a talk, a couple approached me and shared that when they need to have a hard conversation, they find that pirate accents bring their defenses right down. Amazing! Maybe a French accent is more your thing.

- *Role-play.* Many couples experiment with roles as part of stoking the flames of desire in a long-term relationship. Could these alter egos also talk about sex?

- *Speak in the third person.* "She loves it when he goes down on her." "She gets so turned on when she takes charge." Adding a bit of space between you and your words is another pathway for reducing feelings of vulnerability and defensiveness.

Take what you want from this list and leave the rest. Figure out what works for you. As you and your partner cocreate an erotic journey that supports you individually and collectively, choose love over fear again and again.

When your partner shares a want, need, or concern with you, strive to listen deeply. Deep listening is about listening to *understand* instead of listening to *respond*. Deep listening requires that we de-center our own experience and focus on the experience of our partner. Try to really take on your partner's perspective, experiencing the need or concern through *their* lens, not your own. Therapist Paul Brode likens the relationship between speaking and listening to the relationship between a liquid and a bowl. Imagine a liquid that is being poured into a bowl. Speaking is the liquid and listening is the bowl. Your listening constitutes your partner's speaking. When you listen deeply, you hold, contain, and shape that which is being given voice. Deep listening requires practice because it is so different from our default communication style of react and respond. And while deep listening is a generally important relationship skill, because our sexualities are home to deep vulnerability, it is essential when the topic of conversation is sex.

It is so hard not to personalize your partner's sexuality. If your partner is using pornography, you may start to tell yourself a story that you are not hot enough or bold enough. If your partner does not have an orgasm or loses their erection, you may start to tell yourself a story that you are sexually inadequate. You are less likely to lose yourself in a shame-loaded story if you are able to use deep listening to focus your attention on your partner's experience. Your willingness to "be the bowl" increases the chances that what your partner shares will feel authentic (versus full of rationalization, defensiveness, and that which feels to you like "excuses") and makes it more likely that you'll receive the same deep listening in return.

When couples commit themselves to the practice of deep listening, it feels easier and safer to share tender reports from your inner worlds. Our sexualities are so uniquely our own, and when we are given the opportunity to "visit" each other's worlds, we must de-center our own experiences, resist the urge to import our own meanings, and be present with what our partner is sharing.

To Fake or Not to Fake, That Is the Question

In chapter 4, I promised that we would come back to the topic of faking orgasms, and here we are. By now you know the drill. I will not tell you and Your Sexy how to behave, but I will provide you with information and perspective you can use toward empowerment and authenticity. Research indicates that lots of women and some men fake orgasms at least some of the time.[131] Reasons that women give for faking an orgasm include: not wanting to hurt a partner's feelings, wanting to build up a partner's ego, not wanting to feel sexually inadequate, wanting to appear sexy, avoiding conflict, enhancing excitement, and wanting sex to end. Reasons that men give for faking include: wanting to avoid having their partner thinking something is wrong with them, protecting their partner from feeling inadequate or unattractive, covering up for premature ejaculation, intoxication, or having had an orgasm earlier in the day.[132]

People fake orgasms because our stories about sex are so entwined with stories about performance and worth. All too often we act as if an orgasm is a gold star upon our forehead, signifying that we have done a good job. Keep in mind that sex can be pleasurable without having an orgasm. And, because an orgasm is a series of involuntary muscle contractions, you can have one without feeling pleasure, especially if you don't feel cared for or emotionally safe and connected. You do not need to chase an orgasm to be worthy, and great sex is body-centered and pleasure-focused, not narrowly and fearfully focused on one goal.

This pervasive pattern of women faking orgasms is the inevitable consequence of a culture that operates from a sexual script that is rigid, linear, and heterosexually biased, dictating that *she* should orgasm before *he* orgasms and that *her* orgasm is *his* responsibility.

When sex is script-based instead of authentic, the conditions are ripe for misunderstanding. For example, my student Sherri told me a story about a casual sexual experience. Her partner didn't have an orgasm, and he later offered her an apology for his lack of climax.[133] Sherri recalls being caught off guard by his apology because her pleasure had not been diminished even a little. She wondered if perhaps he was projecting onto her what *he* might have felt if the tables had been turned. Because this script holds him responsible for her orgasm, if she hadn't had an orgasm, perhaps he would have felt diminished and embarrassed. So, he assumed she would too. Sigh. Sexual scripts are exhausting.

Faking an orgasm is a miscommunication, one that sends the message that a sex act is "working" when it isn't. One of my students had a clear feminist agenda when she made the commitment to stop faking orgasms, especially during nonrelationship sex. She said, "I realized that if I fake an orgasm, he is going to think that what he did felt good when it didn't. I starting to think about the women he would go on to have sex with after me, and I just decided that I could no longer in good conscience do that to my 'sisters.'"

Faking an orgasm repeatedly with the same partner will keep you from working together to figure out behaviors that *would* be more orgasm-producing for you. As you deepen your connection with Your Sexy, you may be considering letting your partner know that you've been faking orgasms. Disclosing to your partner that you've been faking orgasms may feel to you and/or to your partner like a confession of a betrayal, which is why you both need to remember that *every sexual problem is a couple problem*. Far from being punitive or intentionally hurtful, this disclosure reflects your desire for the two of you to be closer and for your sexual relationship to be as rich and rewarding as possible. Hold self-compassion for the ways in which our culture has set you up not to value your own pleasure *and* hold empathy for the fact that your partner might feel hurt and confused by your disclosure.

Framing your disclosure as a we-issue sounds like this, "I love us, and I want us to enjoy our lovemaking as much as possible. I'm realizing the extent to which I have internalized a bunch of toxic and unhelpful messages about sex, and those messages have kept me from understanding that I deserve to slow down, feel good, and explore the possibility of having an orgasm. Will you work with me to make this different for me and for us?" Your work is to move toward greater integrity by standing up for yourself without putting your partner down. Your partner's work is to hold onto *both* their hurt feelings *and* faith that moving through difficult moments makes couples stronger.

> Return to this sentence stem: *"It is difficult for me to talk to my partner about sex because…"* and write a response to it if you haven't already. What tools or insights from this book could you use to make it easier to talk with your partner about your sexual wants and needs?

Intimacy is the cocreation of meaning and experience.[134] Sex is profoundly personal and profoundly relational at the very same time. Befriending the depth and complexity of Your Sexy helps you meet the depth and complexity of your partner's Sexy. This process is reciprocal and dynamic. Esther Perel writes that for erotically intelligent couples, "Love is a vessel that contains both security and adventure, and commitment offers one of the greatest luxuries of life: time. Marriage is not the end of a romance; it is the beginning. They know that they have years in which to deepen their connection, to experiment, to regress, and even to fail. They see their relationship as something alive and ongoing, not a fait accompli. It's a story they are writing together, one with many chapters, and neither partner knows how it will end. There's always a place they haven't gone yet, always something about the other still to be discovered."[135] Deepening, widening, and sharing sexual self-awareness with a partner is the beautiful and difficult work of a lifetime.

�֍

Your Sexy lives at the intersection of the internal and the relational. Your reward for the deeply personal and difficult work of getting to know Your Sexy is the intimacy you can then cultivate in the space between an empowered you and an attuned partner.

spiritual

Sex as Transcendence

The human body that we have been conditioned to see as a system of chemicals, pulleys, pumps, and plumbing is an expressive entity of great subtlety and nuance. This subtle body is alive, diaphanous, full of meanings, poetic, expressive in every organ and part, intimately connected to emotion and feeling, and, by no means least, beautiful.

—Thomas Moore, *The Soul of Sex*

Spirituality is our final destination on this journey to deepen your connection with Your Sexy. One of the founding mamas of sex therapy, Dr. Gina Ogden, says that we need no further proof of the deep connection between sex and spirituality than the fact that many of us exclaim, "Oh God," at the moment of orgasm. There is, it seems, plenty for us to explore! Our central question here is: *To what degree do your faith-based practices support Your Sexy, and to what degree do your faith-based practices constrain Your Sexy?*

The relationship between sex and spirituality is historical, complicated, and the topic of entire books. Some of us have a closely held, extremely meaningful, and deeply personal relationship with our religion or spirituality. Others of us have no relationship at all. Your spiritual backstory will inform your experience of this chapter. This chapter may hold incredibly important work for you as you reclaim Your Sexy, or it may offer you little to nothing. For one of the members of my writing team, a woman who attended seventeen years of Catholic school, this was by far the most emotionally stirring and transformative chapter. Another member of my team grew up in China with zero faith-based practices, so she struggled to connect with the notion of spiritual transcendence until she identified her relationship with nature as her parallel transcendent pathway.

Each of us has a story of our spirituality, one that is very much worth telling. I want to give you a CliffsNotes version of mine so you know the place from which this chapter is written. I was born and raised with sporadic attendance at a liberal Presbyterian church. I fell in love with the first Jewish man I ever met and joyously converted to reform Judaism when I was twenty-four years old. In college, my favorite place to explore was my campus's local feminist bookstore, which was full of spiritual books of all kinds. Oprah has been my North Star since I was in my twenties, and I have devoured every one of her SuperSoul creations. My best friend since I was ten years old is a shaman whose spiritual gifts are wider than the sky, deeper than the sea, and make-me-cry beautiful. Today, my family and I belong to a synagogue with a strong social justice lens, and, for the past almost ten years, I have been part of a local community of spiritual "seekers." We read spiritual books, meet regularly together to do soul-nourishing work, and attend events together with spiritual teachers of all kinds. When my father died a few years ago, my belief that we remain deeply connected to each other, even in death, eased my grief tremendously.

So, yeah, I cast a wide spiritual net. What I know for sure is that the more that I can hold awareness of the total interconnectedness of everything, the more I feel peaceful, openhearted, brave...and connected to My Sexy. That is the story of my spirituality. As I wrote this chapter, I felt that I was walking on a tightrope, balancing between directive and irreverent, and I am aware that my perspective may run counter to that which you hold dear. So, as you read this chapter, keep a close eye on what stirs in you, trusting that those places where you feel either intrigued or upset hold important clues about your internalized beliefs about spirituality and sex. When you attend to your reactions, you give yourself a beautiful opportunity to choose—deepen the beliefs that serve you and release the ones that do not.

Religious Versus Spiritual

Religion is an "organized belief system that includes shared, institution-alized, moral values, practices, involvement in a faith community, and, for most, belief in God or Higher Power."[136] Being religious is about belonging to an established order like Christianity, Judaism, Islam, Buddhism, or Hinduism. Religious communities use rituals and cere-monies, imbued with meaning and significance, to connect people to each other, to their shared history, and to God or a higher power.

Spirituality is a "dimension of human experience involving tran-scendent beliefs and practices."[137] Spirituality is both the centerpiece of religion and something that can exist outside of formalized religious structures. Some of us use our religious practices as a pathway for experiencing a sense of spirituality. Others of us identify as "spiritual but not religious," meaning that we do not belong to an institutional-ized faith community but find renewal and connection through per-sonal practices perhaps involving prayer, meditation, yoga, nature, art, activism, or service to others.

Spirituality is simply the recognition that you are more than just the body you live in. You are connected to everything, everywhere, always. Some spiritual teachers describe that we are *both* the wave *and* the ocean. Each of us is *both* a unique expression *and* part of a greater whole to which we belong. French philosopher Pierre Teilhard de Chardin wrote, "We are not human beings having a spiritual experi-ence. We are spiritual beings having a human experience."[138]

While spiritual practices are diverse, they hold in common the possibility for *transcendence*—existence or experience beyond the physical world. These practices help us widen our lens as we shift from, "I am a small, individual, imperfect human being," to "I am connected to all that is." Research indicates that spiritual practices, whether they take place in a faith community or in your backyard, benefit our physi-cal and mental health.[139]

Today, more of us than ever seek these benefits in personal rather than formal ways. About 90 percent of Americans say that they believe in God, but their definitions of God tend to be less institutionalized and more personalized.[140] Only about half of the people who believe in God say that they believe in the God described in the Bible, while the rest of the believers support something more akin to a higher power or a spiritual force.[141] Further, a global look at people under forty years old has found that they are significantly less likely to be religiously affiliated than older people, and this finding holds even when today's younger adults are compared with the younger adults of previous generations.[142] The forces behind this trend away from formalized religious communities are multiple and well beyond the scope of this book, but what we know for sure is that a lot of us shifted from religious to spiritual because our religious institutions were offering more shame than solace.

God, Sex, and Shame

Religious institutions have historically been top-down, patriarchal systems, and as such, they have perpetuated notions of male superiority by connecting the masculine with the holy and the feminine with the profane. Nowhere are those messages louder than in the realm of sex.

Most religions place restrictions and conditions on their followers' sexual behavior, creating the conditions for internal conflict between duty and curiosity. And when we push away thoughts or desires we've been told are sinful, they tend to gain power. Sex researcher Dr. Justin Lehmiller found that "people who were religiously affiliated and who, presumably, had the most sexual constraints placed upon them, tended to fantasize more about breaking free of them. Specifically, they were more likely to fantasize about a range of novel and taboo sex acts."[143] Whether these fantasies are troubling or problematic is a separate matter, but this finding serves as a reminder that telling someone something is "bad" does not make it go away.

The traditional religious doctrine is that sex must be one man and one woman for life with sex sanctioned only within the bonds of matrimony. If purity was a prominent focus of your religious upbringing, Your Sexy will benefit from reflection on the lasting echoes of that message. I have spent lots of hours talking with students and clients who grew up in religiously conservative communities. When they tell me that their choice to abstain from sex is challenging for them, it is often the first time they have admitted that out loud. They have internalized a story that abstaining from sex until marriage ought to be a simple, straightforward, and easy reflection of their commitment to God. And when it isn't easy (and you aren't allowed to say it isn't easy), the emotion that emerges is *shame*.

There is also widespread confusion about what exactly delineates being "pure" from being "impure." Research has found that evangelical college students used a range of definitions of abstinence including: waiting until the wedding ceremony to kiss, kissing only while standing up, and "everything but" penis in vagina intercourse including oral and anal sex.[144] This lack of clarity persists because asking the question, "Where is the line?" feels sinful and shameful. In her stirring book, which is one part journalistic examination of the effects of evangelical Christianity's purity culture and one part memoir, Linda Kay Klein writes, "And so we wander into the forest of sexuality without a compass, grabbing hold of whatever trinkets we can find to guide us. Yet if our natural curiosity leads us into an off-limits section of that forest, we are told we should have known—or worse yet, we *did* know—just what we were doing."[145]

The very notion of virginity is fraught. First, it is a profoundly heterosexual construct defined as a penis entering a vagina, obliterating the first sexual experiences of LGBTQ+ individuals. Second, it is an experiential descriptor masquerading as an entire story. Whether you have had the experience of penile-vaginal intercourse is a statement of fact onto which the culture heaps a story about your goodness, morality, and value as a person. Those stories cut both ways, as some people take the fact of their virginity and layer onto it a story about their prudishness or lack of desirability. Further, our language around virginity reinforces problematic and rigid heterosexual scripts. We say that she *gave her virginity* to him, conveying sacrifice. And we say that people *lose their virginity*, as if sexual experience somehow reduces who they once were.

What might the possibilities for intimacy and connection be if everyone could wade mindfully into the waters of sexuality guided by internal and relational cues of readiness (trust, respect, safety, and care) rather than by fear-based frenetic attempts to rid oneself of something shameful or to cling desperately to something that purports to convey worth? I adore feminist Jessica Valenti's proposal that we redefine virginity as the first time you experience an orgasm with a partner.[146] Subversion at its finest!

Another complicated twist is that although both men and women are expected to practice abstinence until marriage, girls and women are often given the added responsibility of ensuring that they do not (accidentally or purposefully) trigger boys' and men's desire. Being taught, often from a young age, that your sexuality is threatening and dangerous is a setup for a complicated relationship with your sexuality. To whom does it belong? What is its power? In the most painful of scenarios, this message also creates the conditions for women to be blamed for the sexual violence that is perpetrated against them.

This knot of religion and sex is beyond complicated, and I am a clinician not a theologian. If you are choosing not to express Your Sexy until and unless you are married to honor a religious code, or for any other reason, and that choice is working well for you, I want to offer two thoughts. First, I'd encourage you to distinguish *expression* from *existence*. Whether you are sexually active or not, Your Sexy still exists, making it vital to have nonjudgmental spaces where you can share the truth of your experience, ask clarifying questions, and feel supported. Second, when you do begin to express Your Sexy in the context of your marriage, be gentle with yourself. Lifelong paradigms do not shift in just one day—albeit a glorious wedding day! To go from sex as sinful to sex as divine is a process and a practice, one which is likely to require time, support, and information.

Choose three of the following sex-related topics and use the Name-Connect-Choose process (described in chapter 2) to explore the outside-in stories you have internalized about that topic and to assess whether you need to write some new inside-out stories that Your Sexy might prefer.

- Nakedness

- Masturbation

- Sexual pleasure

- Talking about sex

- Sex outside of marriage

- LGBTQ+ sex

- Erotica/porn

Spiritual Renovation

A student of mine, Kaela, was raised in a conservative Christian church, and her spirituality is a core aspect of her identity. However, as she moved through college and graduate school, she began to face a growing disconnect. With an ever-expanding feminist and social justice awareness, she became increasingly troubled by her church's attitudes toward marginalized communities. Further, she struggled to reconcile her church's messages about sex with her growing awareness of her sexuality as an essential aspect of herself, one that she wanted to get to know more deeply.

Kaela and I explored together what felt to her like an impossible choice—either repress her concerns or abandon her church (and the familial and community bonds therein). We wondered together about whether she could choose a third path—the renovation of her spiritual home. Her spirituality seemed to need some skylights, a second floor, more room generally to expand. Spiritual renovation may feel disloyal, disrespectful, perhaps even heretical. But that guilt might be assuaged by holding an awareness of a both-and: You can be *both* grateful for your religious upbringing *and* critical of its lingering impact.

If your religious upbringing has left Your Sexy feeling disconnected, controlled, and devalued, consider making some renovations to the "house" of your spiritual beliefs. This process can take all different forms, so I want to focus on the possibility of introducing your sexuality and your spiritualty to each other.

What might it be like to develop a spiritually infused sexuality (or a sexually infused spirituality)? If your mind is flooding with resistance, *This feels sinful, witchy, silly, woo-woo,* just notice that and breathe. How you blend your spirituality and Your Sexy in a way that feels positive, healing, and empowering is for you (and for you and a partner) to figure out. If it feels like you'd be starting from nothing, you are, in fact, far from alone and can lean on the wisdom and practices of those who have come before you, so let's get specific about spiritually infused sexuality.

Sex as a Spiritual Practice

Perhaps you already consider sex to be a spiritual practice, but, for many of us, sex is tied far more closely to sin than redemption. Integrating your sexuality and your spirituality can create profound sexual healing. I sometimes think of spiritual practices as supercharged mindfulness practices. We already know that mindfulness practices will help Your Sexy experience greater sexual pleasure, and many people have found that spiritual practices take sexual experiences to new dimensions.

Spiritual life and erotic life are fertile grounds for exploring *the power of ritual*. Rituals are a series of actions performed according to a prescribed order. Faith communities are grounded in rituals, using food, prayer, clothing, candles, and more to imbue moments with sacred energy and meaning. Rituals transport us from ordinary to special and move us from "me" to "we." When we invite that same sense of ritual into our erotic experiences, we expand the possibilities for connection and pleasure. As the creator of *Urban Tantra*, Barbara Carrellas, explains, "Ritual has been given a really bad rap. Rituals simply focus energy. Your ritual might be brief and simple or long and wildly elaborate…you can create both a ritual and a ritual space that suit your style—and your schedule."[147]

What a paradox that we cue our five senses so we can be transported to an experience that takes us beyond the senses to something big, wide, and timeless. Spiritually based sexual practices like Tantra make a distinction between *pleasure* and *ecstasy*. Mindfulness practices help us experience pleasure. Practices that integrate sexuality and spirituality help us experience ecstasy. Pleasure is a five-sensory experience tied to the nervous system. Ecstasy, by contrast, is not a feeling or sensation. Ecstasy is, as Carrellas explains, "experienced as overwhelming delight and/or inspiration. It can be a rapturous passionate feeling or a mental transport to a place of well-being, peace, or visions. It is a sense of supreme happiness, freedom, and/or transformation felt in and by the soul."[148] Resist the urge to make ecstasy a goal because the pursuit of ecstasy runs counter to its very nature. Instead, see what happens as you feel your way more deeply into a sense of entitlement.

Begin by bringing intentionality to sex in whatever ways call to *you*. See what shifts when you create a space for sex that is imbued with the sacred. Consider candles, music, scents, sensual clothing, props, and affirmations. You may find that ritual calls forth a different aspect of you. The hope is that ritual cues Your Sexy that it is time to shift from the role of student/worker/boss/wife/mother to the role of lover in a permission-giving and healing way.

Sexual intentionality can help couples as well. Making sexual expression into a spiritual practice can help navigate desire discrepancy and responsive desire. If you and your partner agree, for example, that you "worship" on Saturday evenings, this plan can go a long way toward neutralizing the stories that get heaped onto things like who initiates, how, and when. While some people resist the idea of scheduling sex by judging it as unromantic, see what happens if you reframe it as an erotic practice or intimate ritual.

Finally, infusing your sexual experiences with a sense of the sacred can help you transform shame. Through this lens, you—all of you, exactly as you are right now—are a beautiful expression of the divine. Your partner is a beautiful expression of the divine. Your lovemaking is a communion and a celebration. Sexual shame might just wither when met with this kind of love.

This exercise is about connecting, in a symbolic way, with the sacred nature of sexuality.

1. Go for a walk. As you walk, use mindfulness skills to quiet your mind and open up your heart. Engage your five senses, taking note of what you see, feel, hear, taste, and smell.

2. When you feel present, grounded, and openhearted, look around for an object that represents a loving, wholehearted, and authentic expression of Your Sexy.

3. Write a little bit about why you chose that object and what it symbolizes for you.

If you are in an intimate relationship, consider doing some or all of the following:

•   Show your partner the object you chose and talk about what it means to you.

•   Ask your partner to find an object that symbolizes Their Sexy and to tell you about their choice.

•   Walk together and find an object that captures the sexual relationship that the two of you have with each other.

•   Use these objects to create an altar in your home that honors and celebrates your sexualities.

�֍

Spirituality and sexuality have traditionally been held in opposition, with the former treated with reverence and the latter treated with scorn. All too often, religious institutions have acted as yet another purveyor of the message that sexual desire is inherently dangerous, creating the conditions for shame and disconnection. The reclamation of Your Sexy may entail introducing your spirituality and your sexuality to each other and exploring pathways to integration. Spiritually infused sexual practices can offer healing and amplify pleasure and connection.

PART III

Your Sexy Is Here to Stay

11

Your Grandma Never Swiped Right

Almost any separate way of organizing caregiving, childrearing, residential arrangements, sexual interactions, or interpersonal redistribution of resources has been tried by some society at some point in time. But the coexistence in ONE society of so many alternative ways of doing all of these different things—and the comparative legitimacy accorded to many of them—has never been seen before.

—Stephanie Coontz, *Marriage, A History*

As you step into this vibrantly empowered Sexy, using sexual self-awareness to cultivate what you want and need from the inside-out, it's time for us to look at how to navigate the wild and tangled landscape of modern love. Regardless of your current relationship status, this chapter has something in it for you. The *bad news* is that you face challenges and complexities in loving and being loved that previous generations could never have even imagined. The *good news* is that your sexual and intimate relationships are likely to be more egalitarian and personalized than previous generations could have ever hoped for. *In this world of possibilities, sexual self-awareness is a necessity not a luxury.* Your sexual self-awareness is your GPS, guiding you toward choices that are aligned with who you are and what you need, and away from those that drain your energy and dim your light. We'll look at marriage, sexual monogamy, infidelity, pornography, and dating apps. For each of these, we'll identify challenges and opportunities, and talk about how to make wholehearted choices that work for you...and Your Sexy.

Reflect on the "architecture" of the intimate relationships and marriages that are one and two generations above you in your family tree—your parents, aunts, uncles, grandparents, great-aunts, and great-uncles. Write responsively to the following:

- If these elders were or are married, how old were they when they got married? How old were they when they became parents?

- Describe how they enacted or enact the following:

    Division of labor: breadwinning and caretaking

    Gender roles

    Sexual and romantic expression (to the degree that you know)

    Leisure activities

    Traditions

    Finances

    Conflict

    Religious and spiritual practices

- In what specific ways are your romantic relationships *similar to* and *different from* the romantic relationships of the generations before you?

- When you think about the intimate relationships in your family of origin, what are the aspects of those relationships that you would like to carry into your own intimate relationship? Why? What aspects of those relationships would you like to leave behind or transform? Why?

Digital Footprints

It is impossible to overstate how profoundly technology affects how we "do" relationships, and the exponential pace of technological development can leave us all feeling a bit dizzy. When we consider how a given technology shapes our relationships, the impact tends to be a matter of degree versus a wholesale difference.

Technology takes perennial human questions like, "Do I matter to you?" "Are you with me?" "Am I worthy?" and cranks up the intensity. Whether your partner likes and comments on your Instagram post can feel like their answer to the question that you carry (because it's the question that everyone in a relationship carries), "Do I matter to you?" If you comment on your ex-partner's Facebook photo, it might feel to your partner like you are giving them an answer to their question, "Are you with me?" If you are ghosted after a first date, you may ask yourself, "Am I worthy?" Side note: The answer to that question is, "Hell yes, you are worthy!" Ghosting is a reflection that someone is (momentarily or chronically) out of their integrity. It's says everything about them and nothing about you. Be present to the sting created by being ghosted and then move along. The bottom line is that our relationships today exist simultaneously URL (online) and IRL (in real life), generating exponentially more points of potential contact that nurture or erode connection. Modern love is complicated!

From Role-to-Role to Soul-to-Soul

Intimate relationships have shifted from role-to-role to soul-to-soul. Historically, there has been a singular acceptable narrative arc for love: date, marry, have babies. This traditional script is highly gender-bound: one husband marries one wife. And it is highly role-bound: he is the breadwinner, and she is the homemaker. Those who deviated from this script, by choice or by fate, risked consequences for stepping out of line.

Under this role-to-role paradigm, love comes second to duty. In fact, historically, love was considered a far too fleeting basis for something as serious as marriage.[149] Even today, in many parts of the world, it remains common for marriage to begin as a contract arranged, at least in part, by people other than the couple, with the hope that love will follow from commitment. Research indicates that arranged marriages are no less successful than so-called love marriages.[150] Contrast this with the modern Western imagining of intimate partnership, where the expectation that we marry for love is unimpeachable. We expect our intimate partner to be our lover, our best friend, our cheerleader, our co-parent, and sometimes our business partner. Most of us expect intimate partnership and marriage to be founded upon a connection that is soul-to-soul.[151]

This role-to-soul shift is tied to gender, as the lives of women have changed dramatically and quickly.[152] My mother-in-law, who is in her seventies, says that her father used to tell her, "Honey, you can be *anything* you want to be—a nurse or a teacher!" His encouragement was sincere, given that, for him, it was radical to see women heading off to college at all. She is also clear that she went to college primarily to earn her "M.R.S. Degree" (in other words, to find a husband). Fast-forward, and today, girls outpace boys at every level of educational attainment, and women earn three college diplomas for every two earned by men.[153] Men's lives have changed dramatically as well. Traditional models of what it means to be a "good man" cannot survive in this new world, leaving us desperate for new flexible and adaptive definitions of modern masculinity.

Given all of this, it is rather unlikely that you will simply recreate the models of intimate partnership you've seen in your family. Intimacy today is defined as "into me see." We want an intimate relationship strong enough to hold our boldest dreams and flexible enough to adapt to the ever-changing demands of life. This soul-to-soul approach to love is beautiful in its potential to grant each partner both security and freedom. It is also exhausting. In role-to-role connection, there's little need for negotiation, as the structure of the partnership has been predetermined. It's plug and play. But in soul-to-soul connection, the entire architecture of the relationship is up for negotiation, requiring tremendous emotional and mental bandwidth to address questions like:

- Will we get married? Why? When? How?

- Will we be sexually monogamous?

- Whose career aspirations will be prioritized at which points in time?

- Will we have children?

- How will mundane decisions get made? Who stays home from work when the baby is sick?

- How will we help each other continue to evolve into our best selves?

- How will we cope with periods of time when we are less "into" our marriage?

- How will we keep the spark alive?

Loving soul-to-soul is an active process of creation and re-creation. The intimate partnership you need at age twenty-eight is not the same one you need at age forty-eight, and it is not the same one you need at age sixty-eight. Having all those relationships with the same person requires you to embrace the difficult and beautiful work of standing shoulder to shoulder with your partner, exploring again and again how you will honor each partner's wants and needs while also honoring the needs of the "we." Love is a verb, one that we must enact again and again.

Marriage and You

Zoe and Dalia come to therapy to figure out where their relationship is going. Zoe wants to get married. Dalia does not. Although Dalia has explained to Zoe that her resistance to marriage reflects her ideological discomfort with the institution itself, *not* her ambivalence about committing to being with Zoe forever, Zoe struggles to hear Dalia's hesitance as anything other than a personal rejection. Couples like Zoe and Dalia reflect this complicated cultural moment in which there are no easy answers and in which we must use relational self-awareness to discern fear from authenticity, reactivity from choice. Zoe, Dalia, and I begin by looking at their individual relationships with the institution of marriage itself.

Public and Private: The Marital Both-And

The institution of marriage is a both-and: both private and public at the exact same time.[154] Marriage is *both* a (usually) love-based personal decision made by two people *and* a contract between the couple and the county, state, and country in which they live. The *interior* of a marriage is created by the couple—including how they share resources, how they handle conflict (unless there is violence, at which point the public [the police] steps in), and how they balance time together and time apart. The *exterior* of a marriage is a public contract. The terms of marriage are regulated by the government—including who can marry and when, the rights and privileges that accompany the status, and how and when a marriage can be terminated. The public nature of marriage means there is a long history of discrimination against some loving and consenting adults who want to build their lives together.

Interracial marriage was prohibited in some states until 1967. Today, one in six new marriages in the United States crosses racial and/or ethnic lines.[155] Intimate relationships that bridge cultural differences bring both opportunities and stressors. Prejudice remains a strong headwind for intercultural couples, and the pain of marginalization can be especially acute if the couple faces judgment or rejection from their own families. Cultural differences between partners in experience, beliefs, and privilege play out in both clear and subtle ways, but when I ask intercultural couples to talk with me about the impact of their differences, my therapy office is often the first place those conversations occur. This is a clear indication of how much work our society has yet to do in understanding and communicating the impact of racism, xenophobia, and other biases. Talking with curiosity and compassion about your differences deepens intimacy and grows self-awareness.

Same-sex marriage was not legalized in all fifty states until 2015. Beyond the basic human mandate to treat all people with dignity, research has found that being in a *legally recognized* same-sex relationship, marriage in particular, diminished the mental health discrepancy that tends to be found between people who are heterosexual and people who are LGBTQ+.[156] It is wholly unsurprising that when the public affirms your love by granting you and your partner access to the privileges that come with the institution of marriage, you suffer less. As with intercultural couples, LGBTQ+ couples (intercultural or not) may still face the pain of exclusion from their families of origin, seeking belonging and support in *chosen families* comprised of friends and allies. Intimate relationships are hard, and they can feel isolating at times. All couples need and deserve a supportive community to be the wind beneath their wings!

This history looms large for Zoe and Dalia. As a queer couple, the possibility of a legal marriage is new. While Zoe is ready to dive into the rights and privileges that accompany this status, Dalia feels skeptical and judgmental in the face of this institution's troubling history. For Zoe, to marry is to be validated. For Dalia, to marry is to acquiesce. Our work in couples therapy is to resist the urge to make one of these stances "right" and one of these stances "wrong." We must instead sit in this difference and bear witness to the underlying emotions and beliefs that drive each partner's perspective.

Capstone Versus Cornerstone

Zoe and Dalia are in their twenties, and their feelings about marriage are shaped by the generation to which they belong. The rate of marriage in the United States is declining, and people are marrying later than ever.[157] Still, most Americans *will* get married at some point, and most young adults continue to state that they would like to get married.[158] Marriage has gone from being a cornerstone to a capstone.[159] Previously, marriage marked the first step to adulthood. Partners left their parents' homes to create their marital home. Today, people feel they need to get their "ducks in a row" educationally, developmentally, and financially before tying the knot. And, due to complex economic and social factors, the on-ramp to full adulting is longer than it used to be…so much so that we have a new developmental life-stage in between adolescence and adulthood that we call "emerging adulthood."[160] As Jay-Z says, "Thirty is the new twenty."[161]

Rather than simply being a next step that follows organically from love, the decision to get married and the ability to imagine oneself as married are embedded in economic, educational, and cultural realities. Holding this awareness helps partners move from a single story ("Your hesitation is a rejection of me") to a story thick enough to hold these degrees of complexity.

For Zoe and Dalia to move from standoff to collaboration, they need to unpack how differences *between* them shape their relationships with the institution of marriage. Zoe is an African American woman from a wealthy, well-educated, and religiously conservative family, and Dalia is a white woman from a working-class family. Social location and degree of privilege shape what each of them imagines as possible and preferable for their lives. It is through gentle and empathic conversation that Dalia opens up to Zoe about her "survivor guilt." She is the first in her family to go to college, and she is building a life with a level of security (both economic and emotional) not found in her family of origin. Dalia's anti-marriage stance highlights her longstanding struggle with an *invisible loyalty*—an unconscious agreement she carries not to threaten her connection to her family of origin by "outdoing" them.[162] Many of us carry an invisible loyalty question that sounds like this: "Can I thrive and still belong here?"

The Children of Love's Disillusioned

The rate of divorce crept up throughout the twentieth century, peaked in the 1970s and early 1980s, and has been decreasing ever since.[163] Divorce is therefore a somewhat normative experience for those who belong to Gen X, Gen Y, or Gen Z. Living through the pain of your parents' divorce (or even just experiencing the pain vicariously through friends or extended family) can leave you with fears about your ability to make a marriage last.

Although some data indicate that the kids of divorced parents may face an increased risk of divorce, I have found that the kids of divorced parents are often *more* motivated to commit themselves to a journey of relational self-awareness that pays dividends in the form of greater relationship satisfaction.[164] The relationship between parental divorce and the durability of your romantic relationship is complicated, and some data suggest that two factors really matter: conflict management and commitment to marriage.[165] These two factors are related: the better able you are to weather the inevitable rough patches of long-term love, the easier it is to feel "at home" in the relationship and energized about doing all the fun stuff that makes commitment feel like a gift, not a chore!

Zoe and Dalia have very different relational inheritances here as well. While Zoe was surrounded by loving marriages in her extended family, Dalia witnessed a lot of relational pain. In therapy, we work to discern the degree to which Dalia's stance against marriage is her deepest truth versus a way to protect her from an understandable fear.

Dissolving a power struggle like the one between Dalia and Zoe is a two-person effort. Zoe needed to take responsibility for the ways in which her privileges generated in her both a sense of impatience and a feeling that her way was the "right way." The more she positioned herself in this one-up stance, the more Dalia dug into her rigid belief that marriage is for people who can't think for themselves. And Dalia needed to courageously unpack the baggage she carried into her relationship. Although she hadn't asked for that baggage, it was hers to address nonetheless. Naming the baggage and connecting to the pain helped her shed old coping strategies and choose love. The postscript to this story is that Zoe and Dalia's courageous work resulted in them deciding to get married—a choice that both of them experienced as a cocreation, not a capitulation.

More Than Two

Consensual nonmonogamy (CNM) is not a novel concept. Dossie Easton and Janet Hardy published their definitive guide to CNM, *The Ethical Slut*, in 1997![166] What *is* novel is that CNM is moving from the margins to the mainstream, challenging the dominant discourse that sexual monogamy is the normal, natural, and superior way to do love. Between 2006 and 2015, Google searches for polyamory and open relationships increased—and did so in a manner that was unique to those terms rather than reflective of increased Google searching in general.[167] And a 2016 YouGov poll found that nearly half of Millennials stated that their ideal romantic relationship would be somewhere between completely monogamous and completely nonmonogamous, with those under thirty being most likely to be open to sexual nonmonogamy.[168]

Far from a free-for-all, couples who practice CNM must work together to create and enact agreed-upon boundaries (for example, only during travel or only with a member of the friend group) so individual sexual expression is enhancing, rather than damaging. If the couple's agreement is broken, it is a betrayal like any other that must be addressed.

I am far less interested in conversations about which forms of coupling are "better" and which forms are "worse" and far more interested in supporting people choosing a relational boundary that brings out the best in each partner. Rely on your sexual self-awareness to discern whether, when, and under what circumstances CNM would make sense for your life. CNM is best chosen from love, not fear. In other words, CNM is best chosen from a place of awareness and integrity, not simply to placate your partner.[169] Use the books listed in "Additional Resources for Your Sexy" to help you determine if CNM is a healthy choice for you.

What is most exciting to me about CNM coming out of the shadows is this: when sexual monogamy moves from a default to a choice, *all* couples are reminded that sexual boundaries need to be created, clarified, and respected. When CNM is an item on a menu, you and your partner must engage in an intentional, conscious, and joint decision-making process about the sexual boundaries that are going to work for each of you. Whether you opt for CNM or agree to practice sexual monogamy, the process itself will help you know yourself and your partner more deeply. By creating a relational ethic together, you both can lean into the consequences of whatever choice you make.

Equal Opportunity Betrayal

Caroline and her colleague Joe met for a quick drink after work to celebrate the deal they just closed. Although Caroline was in a serious and sexually monogamous relationship with someone else, her attraction toward Joe grew as they began messaging each other and swapping stories about frustration and boredom at home. By the time Caroline appeared in my office for individual therapy a few months after that celebratory beer, she and Joe were involved in a full-fledged emotional and sexual affair. As Caroline told me her story, she said what I have heard so many others say, "I can't believe I am in this situation! I didn't think it could happen to me."

Despite the rise of these alternatives to sexual monogamy, nonconsensual nonmonogamy (aka cheating!) remains a painful possibility. Few topics spike our anxiety quite as much as the topic of infidelity. At the heart of infidelity is a *boundary violation*—a secretive relationship with some blend of emotional intimacy and sexual alchemy. It tends to be a slope we slide down over time, a series of small choices that create a big problem, as the story of Caroline and Joe highlights. While cheating is as old as monogamy, there are three majorly modern twists:

1. Women have filled the cheating gender gap, with research indicating that women today are about as likely to cheat as men.[170]

2. Digital technology makes it easier to cheat, and easier to get caught.

3. More behaviors fall under the umbrella of cheating. Is watching webcam porn cheating? Is communication with someone in a sexual chatroom cheating?[171]

Adding to the complexity, relationship boundaries can be somewhat idiosyncratic. Texting with an ex-partner may feel "normal" to one partner and like a betrayal to another. What about flirting? Dancing at a club with someone other than your partner? Partners can end up in troubled water simply because they haven't talked about what's in-bounds and out-of-bounds.

In our highly romanticized culture, talking directly and in great detail about how each of you defines cheating can itself feel like a betrayal…like you are somehow breaking the spell. In fact, you are writing a different kind of fairy tale, one in which intimacy is cocreated by defining, intentionally and verbally, who you and your partner are to each other. What could be more romantic than two people ensuring that they are building a foundation of integrity and care?

Soul-to-soul love requires us to move from *external guardrails* to *internal guardrails*. In the role-to-role paradigm, the threat of severe consequences (a scarlet letter, violence, death) led women to suppress the urge to cheat (external guardrail). Today, although fear of consequences may keep us "in line," we also need internal guardrails like:

- imagining the hurt that a particular choice would create in your partner

- cultivating a sense of your own integrity, such that sneaking around would feel like a betrayal of who you pride yourself in being

- exploring what the urge to transgress might be trying to tell you ("I feel bored," "I want to end this relationship but don't know how," "I am acting out because I carry unaddressed and unhealed trauma")

- reminding yourself that we can feel attracted to someone without acting on it; a woman's fantasy world is nobody else's business!

If you wonder whether you are on a slippery slope toward cheating, a helpful gut check is to imagine someone is recording the interaction between you and the person you're attracted to and the video will be shown to your partner. How would you feel about your partner seeing it?

Here's the thing though. Even when you are in love and committed to the practice of sexual monogamy, chances are high that you will continue to feel attracted to people who are not your partner. Attraction is amplified by the energies of temptation and transgression. Make peace with the fact that loving someone does not negate the potential for other attractions, because the more you can reckon with all the complicated stirrings within you, the easier it is to make choices that keep you in your integrity. Practicing relational self-awareness means moving from reaction to reflection. Connecting curiously and compassionately to the "data" of your thoughts, feelings, and yearnings will help you choose next steps that you can feel good about.

24-7 Porn

My husband, Todd, and I were in the car listening to the eighties radio station (his choice, not mine. I'm a nineties girl!) when a real throwback came on: "Touch Me" by Samantha Fox. Todd reminded me that at the peak of her celebrity, she posed as the centerfold in *Penthouse* magazine. Apparently, Todd and his teenaged crew were beside themselves with curiosity, but getting your hands on pornography in 1987 required some serious effort. I was laughing so hard as he recounted the many cafeteria conversations they devoted to figuring out how to make their dreams come true. Whose dad might have a copy? Where would it be hidden? How could they steal it without getting caught?

Today, we can grab our phones and, in a matter of seconds, indulge our pop star fantasies. Therapists, researchers, and lovers alike are scrambling to figure out how 24-7 free streaming pornography impacts our sexuality. Rather than being pro-porn or anti-porn, consider the risks and benefits so you and Your Sexy can make the choice to either enjoy erotica guilt-free or forgo from a place of integrity. Your internal clarity will also help you figure out how you want to relate to a partner's use of porn.

Unhelpful Aspects of Porn

Porn can shape our expectations about sex in limiting and unhelpful ways by promulgating misinformation and unrealistic notions like:

- women are always wet on demand with no need for foreplay or lube

- women orgasm loudly, forcefully, and in no time flat from penetration alone

- men are and should be in control of the pace of sexual experiences, and they know exactly what their partners want without asking

- gagging, choking, or otherwise rough behavior without consent or conversation beforehand is common and pleasurable

- men's penises are huge, hard, and able to thrust without ejaculation for a really long time

- women's bodies are flawless, hairless, and fit.

Further, if we are consuming porn that hyper-focuses on mechanics, performance, and orgasm, we may forget that amazing sexual experiences are much less about being "good in bed" and much more about together cultivating joy, play, and connection.

Helpful Aspects of Porn

Porn can be a gateway toward greater sexual self-awareness. Representation matters. If your sexuality was not integrated into the sex education you received, erotic materials that honor bodies like yours and sexualities like yours are like salve on a wound. You may have needed to rely on porn to give you the information you needed at a time when you had nowhere else to turn. Also, porn normalizes sexuality and offers a community of those with similar fantasies and interests. Porn gives people a chance to fantasize about what they may not want to enact in real life. Porn can also reduce pressure on partners to fulfill all of each other's sexual needs. Finally, for those with responsive sexual desire, erotic materials may provide a helpful jumpstart.

Conscious Consumption

A colleague of mine was working with a heterosexual couple, and the male partner came to session complaining that the sex they were having didn't look like porn sex. Not missing a beat, the therapist responded, "What would you say if your kid came home complaining that school is lame because it's not Hogwarts?!" Real-world sex and porn sex are very different beasts. The make-believe world of porn holds both the power to hurt us, by amplifying the message that our bodies exist merely for the pleasure of another, and the power to help us, by opening us to new possibilities for how we might inhabit our sexuality.

Your work is the work of discernment. Be a conscious consumer of erotica:

- Stay mindfully attuned to whether the erotic materials you are using leave you feeling better or worse about yourself.

- Do what you can to ensure you aren't contributing to toxic aspects of the porn industry by choosing ethical and feminist pornography in which adult film actors are safe and fairly compensated for their work.

- Talk with your partner about the role you both would like porn to play in in your relationship; strive for curiosity; remember that that there are three sexualities in your relationship (mine, yours, ours); and get help from a therapist if you are stuck in a place of judgment and hurt.

Swipe Right for Love

Humans have long used intermediaries in their quest for love. Back in the day, it was matchmakers. Then it was personal ads in newspapers. Today, it's apps. Some people lament the loss of the "meet cute"— rather than catching each other's eye at a party, the story becomes,

"They swiped right, and then I swiped right!" But that stigma is quickly dissipating. Most Americans, 59 percent, report that online dating is a good way to meet people, and that number is up from 44 percent in 2005.[172] In fact, about one-third of marriages today are between people who met online, and there's no evidence that those marriages have any better or worse chance of success than couples who met the old-fashioned way.[173] Here again, rather than debating whether swiping for love is good or bad, let's focus on self-aware app usage.

Be realistic. Dating apps have gotten super specific: there's one designed for Disney lovers (MouseMingle) and another for hot sauce lovers (Hot Sauce Passions). It might be tempting to map out compatibility in such a fine-grained way, but research indicates that when people are flooded with options, they become indecisive and less satisfied with the choices they make, a phenomenon that psychologist Barry Schwartz calls the "paradox of choice."[174] Choice is empowering, but if you find yourself feeling restless and constantly wondering who might still be out there, remember there's no such thing as a perfect match. Love is imperfect and fueled by mystery and paradox.

Be compassionate. It is overwhelming to think that every swipe could potentially lead you to your soulmate, and that belief can create heavy pressure to "succeed." It can also leave you feeling like you are failing if you are struggling to connect in this sea of possibilities. Practice self-compassion by putting clear limits on your dating app usage. For example, use your dating app(s) once a day for a predetermined amount of time, and go do something else if and when you start feeling anxious and self-critical. Related to this, be kind to yourself by removing the expectation that the first date must be mind-blowing. Connection takes time and intention to build, so be gentle (toward yourself and your date) about awkward pauses. Everything that is endearing about you won't all show up on the first date...and your date will need time to unfold too.

Be calm. Just because you can Google-stalk the heck out of someone before you meet them doesn't mean you should. Check in with yourself about what's driving your desire to know them before you know them.

Often this is fueled by anxiety like wanting to compare yourself to their last partners. Preemptive Googling may temporarily take the edge off your nerves, but see if you can instead name the anxiety and reframe it as curiosity and excitement. Because we don't get to selectively numb feelings, if you tamp down your anxiety, you also tamp down your enthusiasm.

Be present. Some research indicates that it's helpful to transition as quickly as possible from screen-to-screen communication to face-to-face communication.[175] Plus, drawn-out dating app conversations with multiple people can lead you to feel burnt-out. If you decide based on someone's profile that you'd like to see them in person, be honest and tell them that. Protect your energy and be intentional.

A uniquely modern step on the path to relationship commitment is taking your dating apps off your phones. A graduate student of mine shared a sweet story with me in which she and her girlfriend created an app-deletion ritual involving candles and wine. New partners must create a "container" to cultivate connection and closeness. You need to trust that your partner will not start swiping at the first sign that you aren't exciting enough, chill enough, whatever enough for them. And your new partner needs the same. These steps of commitment may feel scary, but they create the conditions for the vulnerability that makes intimate partnership feel so good.

Dating apps are best considered a means to an end—an avenue for creating in-person interaction. Even if you're using dating apps, cultivating skills, like making small talk and flirting, is good for you. And, dating apps can foster a "consumer mentality" in which we are at risk of treating people as expendable. The sense that there are endless options out there can make us want to "upgrade" at the first hint of frustration or disappointment—a process that quells our anxiety or reduces our irritation in the moment but that also keeps us from leaning into the vulnerability needed to build intimate connection. Your empowered Sexy knows how to ask for what she needs, bringing kindness and clarity to a dating climate that often lacks both.

In what specific ways do you find that technology enhances your romantic relationships? In what ways do you find that technology constrains, limits, or worsens your romantic relationships? Do you need to make some tweaks to your relationship with your technology that might be helpful to your romantic relationships? If so, write a bit about what you might want to change and why.

In order to meet the complexities of modern love, self-awareness is mandatory, not optional. The digital age dangles before us the allure of constant connection, but intimacy demands something different— our presence and attention. The work you've done in this book will help you know and articulate, from the inside-out, what your boundaries are, and this will help you tolerate the "not knowing" that is inherent in intimate relationships. The more you can trust yourself to let someone into your world, emotionally and sexually, at a pace that feels good to you, the less you need to rely on signs (like feeling fireworks on the first date) or rules (sleeping together on the third date) or information (a thorough Google-stalk). With a newly deepened connection to Your Sexy, you can chart a course that serves you—body, heart, and soul.

✳

A lousy intimate relationship wreaks havoc on your life, and a happy one adds vitality, richness, and meaning. What matters most is not how you meet your love or what form your love takes. What matters most is the *how*—how each of you shows up for love. Modern love requires mindfulness and conscious choice. Choose a lifelong practice of relational self-awareness, and choose a partner who similarly values love as a process of reflection and cocreation.

Reflections for Men Who Love Women Who Are Taking Sexy Back

She fell in love with the parts of him that were imperfect, because they reminded her she could be imperfect too.

—Mark Groves, @createthelove, Instagram, May 13, 2015

Dear Reader,

Relationships are systems, and when you make a change in one part of the system, you shake up the entire system. I am guessing you want to share the hard work you've done in this book with the people you love. Because sexuality and gender are so entwined, some conversations are likely easier than others. If you're sharing this book with friends or lovers who are women (or who have been socialized in the feminine), these conversations might flow rather organically. If you're sharing this book with friends or lovers who are men (or who have been socialized as masculine), I'm envisioning that it might be helpful to have some support as conversations about sex that traverse the gender divide can be a bit fraught.

This is a stand-alone chapter you can give to a man you'd like as your ally. Perhaps it will inspire him to read the whole book, but even if he doesn't, this chapter is an invitation into new conversations and experiences that will help Your Sexy feel loved and whole. Unpacking this material together might stir some strong emotions, especially if a dialog like this is new for one or both of you. Lead with love, trust the process, and let go of the outcome.

Love,
Alexandra

If you are a man who is reading this chapter, it is likely because a woman you love—your girlfriend, your wife, your friend—handed it to you. Welcome! She must trust you a lot, because she's inviting you into some stuff that's pretty darned vulnerable.

This book is a journey that guides women toward a deeper and more empowered experience of their sexuality. Sexuality is about far more than a person's sexual orientation or what they do with their genitals. Your sexuality is your sexual self, capturing your entire, complicated, and ever-evolving relationship with the erotic world. It is about how you experience pleasure, trust, play, power, surrender, touch, connection, giving, and receiving. In this book, we refer to sexuality as "Your Sexy." And, while we're defining our terms, in this book, we take an expansive definition of the word "sex"—inclusive of but not limited to penis-in-vagina intercourse.

Our culture inundates all of us with problematic, conflicting, and gendered messages (from parents, teachers, coaches, religious figures, media, the porn industry…the list goes on) about who we should be sexually. These messages tend to leave girls and women feeling as if they are walking a razor's edge between being perceived as a prude and being perceived as a slut. The problem with internalizing noisy messages from the outside world is that you can't really hear yourself. You risk becoming disconnected from your own truths about what feels authentic and good to you. This book invites women to move from an *outside-in* experience of their sexuality (focusing on what everyone else wants and expects from them) to an *inside-out* experience of their sexuality (cultivating a sexuality that feels authentic and aligned to them).

The woman who handed you this chapter is claiming a part of herself that maybe never felt like it belonged to her in the first place. She may still be struggling to figure out when and how to ask for what she needs (in the bedroom and outside of it). And I'm guessing she would love your compassion and your patience as she sorts this out. *Your willingness to be an ally is huge.* The way forward for all of us is to look *together* at the harmful messages we *all* have internalized about sex, so we can forge new possibilities for healthy sexuality and for sexual experiences that are wholehearted, joyful, and empowering.

As you read this chapter, pay attention to what gets stirred up inside of you—feelings of interest, frustration, excitement, sadness, or whatever. Your internal reactions are meaningful data points, and they have a lot to teach you. The more curious and compassionate you can be about what makes you tick as a person, the more open you will be to hearing about the experiences of the people you care about. That's *relational self-awareness*, and it's the cornerstone of happy and healthy relationships.

Being an Ally Means Holding Space

Supporting a woman who is taking Her Sexy back is all about *holding space*. Holding space means being a calm, present, and openhearted witness to someone else's exploration. Instead of rescuing someone from their pain, you listen to their pain. Instead of solving someone's problems, you inquire about them. Instead of explaining what you think is happening, you simply reflect back to that person what you're seeing and hearing.

If the two of you were musicians, you would be the one holding the steady bass beat, and she would be the one riffing. Far from being a passive role, holding space is an active and powerful kind of engagement. And, far from being superfluous, when you are willing to hold space, you are helping her get to know herself more deeply while also deepening trust and connection between the two of you.

Gendered Stories That Need to Go

If you, your father, and grandfather were to have a conversation about the stories each of you has internalized about what it means to be a man, there would likely be significant, and fascinating, differences between the three of you because our culture is evolving with respect to gender role socialization. But these old stories are pervasive and sneaky. For example, a male client said to me recently, "In my head, I know that it's okay to let my wife support me when I'm having a hard time, but it still just feels wrong somehow. I just feel like I should be able to handle stuff on my own."

Be willing to look at the gendered stories you have internalized (in this example, the story is "men shouldn't ask for help") so you can ask yourself whether any given story makes you feel more connected to, or more distant from, the people you care about. Some of the stories our culture foists upon boys and men (heterosexual and LGBTQ+ alike) can make it seem like holding space is awkward or "unmanly." I want to highlight three especially unhelpful stories our culture has told you that might make it harder for you to support the woman in your life as she steps more fully into her sexuality.

Problematic Story #1: Men Should Have It All Figured Out

One of the most toxic stories that our culture tells boys and men is this: *if you are confused, it means you are weak.* The old stereotype that "real men" don't ask for directions (now rendered obsolete by smartphones) reflects this damaging but lingering message that guys must be independent, self-assured, and in charge at all times.

One of the men in my lab interviewed some of the guys in his life about their questions and frustrations regarding women and sex. What stood out most to him wasn't the questions they had about women's sexuality. *It was how badly they felt even having questions at all.* They felt embarrassed that there was stuff they didn't know, and their confusion made them feel inadequate.

Rather than viewing your confusion as a problem, lean into it. *Confusion fuels curiosity.* And curiosity is one of the most potent tools of connection available to human beings. Seek understanding of the experiences of the person you're trying to support by getting curious, asking questions, and listening. Challenge yourself to get comfortable with confusion, trusting it to lead you to the exact places you need to go. Your curiosity is an asset.

Unfortunately, many men feel (consciously or unconsciously) like they need to take this "I have it all figured out" story into the bedroom, putting immense pressure on themselves to be totally confident and in charge. Inside your head, this might sound like you telling yourself that you must perform like a porn star—easily getting and keeping an erection and knowing without asking what it takes to give your partner an orgasm. Shedding this unhelpful story will help you show up as present and curious. You will take a whole lot of pressure off yourself and your partner and open the door for sex to be a playful and intimacy-deepening experience for you both.

A female student in my lab was telling me that she and her friends don't feel able to communicate with male partners about what feels pleasurable to them and what they know to be true about their vulvas and their orgasms because they are afraid of being seen as too assertive or sexually demanding. Only half kidding, she said, "I just don't understand why we can't teach that every vulva is different, and you need to meet a vulva on that vulva's terms." I'm all in on that vision for sex education!

In the meantime, being open to your partner's communication (and guidance) is an amazing place to start. But also know that even when a man is curious instead of assumptive, a woman may not know right away exactly what feels good to her. And she may feel embarrassed or impatient that she needs some time and space to explore her body's responses. The more he can hold a steady and sure space, the braver she will feel to play and express Her Sexy. Put aside scripts from porn or from previous sexual interactions and instead cocreate a sexual journey. Trust that being a great lover is about authenticity, presence, and care.

Problematic Story #2: Men Should Not Be Complicated

Right next to the problematic story that men shouldn't be confused lives an equally problematic story: *men are emotionally simple.* Sit down with a group of parents, and it won't be long before you hear the statement that is like nails on a chalkboard to me: "Boys are so much simpler/easier/less drama than girls!" *The internal emotional worlds of boys and men are no less emotionally complicated than the internal emotional worlds of girls and women.* What this toxic story does is lay the groundwork for a massive cover-up. When boys internalize the story that they are emotionally simple, they end up telling themselves (consciously or unconsciously), "My feelings are messy, abnormal, and unwelcome."

Men learn early on to mask vulnerable feelings like sadness, fear, and shame. As therapist Terry Real says, "For too many men, the only strong emotions they permit themselves are either anger or lust."[176] We all participate in this cover-up. Moms often subtly (or not so subtly) push their sons away for fear of raising a so-called mama's boy. Girlfriends and wives tend to convey a confusing message to their boyfriends and husbands: show me your emotions but also don't turn into a puddle because that scares me. All of us, wittingly and unwittingly, reinforce rigid gender notions that cut each sex off from the possibility of living wholeheartedly.

Allow the people you love to hold space for you. The truth of the matter is, if you're having a hard time, the people who love you probably already know you're struggling because even if you're not talking about it, they can observe it in your behavior. For example, your "tell" may be that you're irritable or withdrawn. So, turning toward people who are trustworthy and letting them know what's going on ends up being an act of kindness, validating the hunch they already have. Far from weakness, letting people be near you when you are hurting is indicative of strength and emotional maturity. And, far from selfish, letting people into your internal world strengthens the bond between you and the people who matter to you. It is a wonderful gift that makes relationships stronger. Our friends and partners tend to judge us far less harshly than we judge ourselves, so I predict that when you let your people hold space for you, you will be pleasantly surprised by the warmth and care they have for your struggle.

Problematic Story #3: Men Need to Prove Themselves Again and Again

In addition to prohibitions against being curious or complicated, our culture tells men this story: *You cannot ever be content.* Sociologist Michael Kimmel says that, in our culture, men are given the message that they need to prove themselves again and again, and this hustle generates pervasive and unyielding anxiety.[177] We talk about men losing their "man card" for doing things associated with femininity. We have the word *emasculated*, but there is no parallel word for women. Femininity is ascribed. Masculinity is achieved. And, therefore, it can be lost, putting men on a hamster wheel, scrambling to feel as though they measure up.

This limiting story fuels anxiety in men and turns women into both coconspirators and collateral damage. Women have been known to use this toxic story in the heat of battle with men, leveling a below-the-belt comment like: "You're not a real man!" Women also fear doing or saying anything that will trigger feelings of inadequacy in men. Nowhere does this play out more powerfully than in the bedroom, where men are supposed to perform—*get* an erection, *maintain* an erection, and *give* mind-blowing orgasms. Paradoxically, the more tied a man is to the message that his manliness rests upon what he does to and with a woman sexually, the more his partner's needs will go unmet because he is losing himself in this story instead of connecting with her.

The story that you need to prove yourself fuels a sense that your value depends on your ability to solve problems, accomplish goals, and fix stuff (like your partner's negative feelings). *What would be different for you if you believed to your core that just being present was enough?* I invite you to trust that your empathy heals. Your presence empowers. Show up. See her. Let her see you.

The Ally's Toolbox

Supporting a woman who is taking Her Sexy back requires you to hold space, so let's get more specific about the tools required to get that job done. These tools are: self-reflection, inquiry, listening, and regulation.

Self-Reflection: Do Your Work

Because our culture's messages about sex are inextricably bound with our culture's messages about gender, you have also internalized lots of problematic stories about who you ought to be as a sexual person, what you ought to want from sex, and how you ought to behave sexually. You likely also have a rather fraught relationship with Your Sexy! *The more willing you are to explore and understand your sexual self, the more you will be able to support the woman who handed you this chapter.*

Sex therapist Doug Braun-Harvey laments the fact that men often need to pay a high price before they can seek a deepened understanding of their sexuality.[178] For many men, it is only once they are in treatment for being victims or perpetrators of sexual abuse or for struggling with a sex addiction that they can finally ask the question: *Who am I sexually?* Men deserve time and space to cultivate sexual self-awareness. Men need to reflect on their sexuality when they are not turned on. If the only time you are in touch with your sexuality is when you are having sex or watching porn, your story about your sexuality is likely far too narrow—focused only on what turns you on and what turns you off. Here are some questions to expand your sexual self-awareness:

- What was the sex education you received when you were young? Looking back on how you learned about sex, what impact does that have on you today?

- How easy or difficult is it to talk with a partner about sex (for example, asking for what you want, asking your partner what they want, checking in, talking about it after)?

- What are the thoughts and feelings you have about your body? How do these thoughts and feelings impact how you feel sexually?

- In your opinion, what is the role of sex in an intimate relationship?

- What are the ingredients for a good/positive/fun sexual experience? (What's happening before, during after? What's your mood? What your partner's mood? How are you feeling about yourself? Your partner?)

The coolest thing about your sexuality is that you don't have to have it all figured out right now. Your sexual self will evolve and change as you do. Understanding and honoring your sexuality is the work of a lifetime.

Inquiry: Lead with Love

What a privilege it is when someone asks us to be their ally and wants to share their story with us! On a topic as charged as sex, sometimes getting the ball rolling is the hardest part. The mere presence of this book in your life might be enough to get you talking together, and sharing your reactions to this chapter can be a gateway to deeper dialog. The woman who handed you this chapter would probably love for you to ask her what she has learned. *Inquiry is loving.* If getting started feels challenging, consider asking her some of these questions:

- What were the stories that you internalized about sex when you were young?

- What were your early sexual experiences like?

- What helps you feel more connected to your sexuality?

- What makes you feel less connected to your sexuality?

- When do you feel most supported by me?

Talking about sex gets easier the more you do it, and the most important thing is to be gentle with yourself and each other.

Listening: Cross the Bridge

Holding space for the woman in your life to unpack her insights and discoveries requires more listening than talking, but, crazy as it may seem, listening is a skill that few of us ever learned. Often, although it appears we are listening, we are actually formulating our response. *Instead of listening to respond, practice listening to understand.* De-center your experiences and your reactions and focus on what she's saying.

Allow yourself to *feel into* whatever she is describing. Let empathy be your guide. Imagine yourself in her shoes and respond from that place. Empathy is conveyed nonverbally with our body posture and face—nodding, leaning in, looking at each other. Empathy is also conveyed with our words.

- If she's sharing something from her past, you might say something like: "You were really brave." "You must have been scared." "You handled a hard situation well." "That sounds awful/amazing/challenging/sad."

- If she's sharing something that she's currently struggling with, you might say something like: "Can you help me understand that better?" "I'm so glad you're talking to me about this." "I want to support you." "I'm listening."

The stories Her Sexy needs to tell might be hard to hear. If she survived trauma or abuse, her story will surely break your heart. *See if your broken heart can, in fact, be a broken-open heart.* You will need to hold onto *both* your rage about what she survived *and* your faith in her recovery. In her reclamation, she must hold onto both her pain and her resilience, and when you can also do that, you multiply the healing by the power of two.

Regulation: Resist Defensiveness

Conversations about sex can go off the rails because the topic stirs enormous vulnerability and self-consciousness. If the woman you are supporting is also your intimate partner, it may be especially challenging for you to resist the urge to explain your behavior or defend yourself because the stakes are so high. Imagine your partner telling you, "It's hard for me to focus on my own pleasure when I feel like you're rushing to get to the intercourse part." You may want to say something like, "Why haven't you have told me that before now?" or "How is that my fault?" or "Then speak up!" Those responses are understandable.

They are also defensive and unhelpful. Her job is to advocate for what she needs without blaming you or putting you down. Your job is to stay open and curious, resisting the urge to debate her. And vice versa when *you* want or need to give *her* some feedback. Your job is to speak up without putting her down, and her job is to remind herself that you are on the same team.

Defensiveness feels like wanting to explain yourself, provide counter-examples, or minimize the other person's feelings. *Because we socialize boys and men to equate standing up for themselves with strength, listening without defensiveness can feel like letting someone walk all over you.* In fact, listening without defensiveness shows that you care, and it builds trust and connection.

If you start to feel defensive, take a deep breath and return your focus to what she's saying (versus on what you want to disagree with or explain). You also might find it helpful to imagine your defensiveness as a shield, one that you put up to protect yourself, but one that you can lay down to connect.[179] Think about your defensiveness as your teacher. *Whatever you're feeling defensive about is tied to a wound, a longing, or a pain point inside of you that is worthy of your attention.*

Also know that, at another time, it would be brave and beautiful to talk with her about the defensiveness you had been feeling: "When you were talking to me about wanting me to run my hands over your body more before we start having sex, I noticed myself starting to feel really defensive." Share with her whatever stories hide out behind your defensiveness—for example, fear of letting her down or self-criticism. Moving from defensiveness to authenticity makes relationships healthier and happier.

Embrace Imperfection

Relationships are dances. A change you make in your part of the dance—from assuming to asking, from silence to voice, from defensive to open, from explaining to listening—will change the entire dance. I hope this chapter encourages you to try out some sweet new moves. Your new moves don't have to be perfect, because the most magnificent part about relationships is that we don't need to be perfect to be worthy of them. Your authentic desire to be an ally matters so much more than your ability to "get it right." Getting it right is an illusion anyway. This aphorism, often attributed to Maya Angelou or Carl W. Buehner, is good one to remember in a situation like this: "I've learned that people will forget what you said, people will forget what you did, but people will never forget how you made them feel."[180] Your kind presence holds the power to help your partner feel cherished. Don't ever underestimate the power of letting people know how much they matter to you. I celebrate the courage it takes to change the conversations we have about sex. Thank you for reading.

13

Welcome Home, Sexy

A woman in harmony with her spirit is like a river flowing. She goes where she will without pretense and arrives at her destination prepared to be herself and only herself.

—Maya Angelou, @DrMayaAngelou, Twitter, January 5, 2019

You and Your badass Sexy made it to the last chapter! You took a journey that required courage and creativity. One that required you to confront a lot of hard stuff. Our world seems hell-bent on silencing and controlling women's sexuality, and you've been absorbing toxic messages about who and how you are supposed to be since you were a little girl. Nevertheless, you chose this book. Whether you discovered *Taking Sexy Back* on your own or it was recommended to you by a therapist, relative, friend, or intimate partner, *you* are the one who has done the work. *You* have expanded your sexual self-awareness. *You* have pushed back against dangerous and deceptive stories until you could declare, with clear eyes and an open heart, "My Sexy is mine to imagine, create, and recreate." *You* have taken Your Sexy back.

The journey toward greater sexual self-awareness is about moving away from fear and toward love. When sex is shrouded in *fear*, shame, pain, misinformation, and silence flourish. When sex is infused with *love*, healthy boundaries, mutuality, respect, and pleasure flourish. You explored so you could courageously *name* the places where fear's grip was strong—inside of you, in the space between you and an intimate partner, and within the larger culture, like family, media, and religious institutions. You allowed yourself to *connect* with the impact of fear-loaded stories about sex, feeling into that oh-so-understandable shame, sadness, and anger. You awakened your ability to *choose* something else on behalf of Your Sexy—something more authentic and aligned, something kinder and more alive.

This self-aware space is your new home. We think of home as the place we came from, but we need to reimagine home as a place we get to create for ourselves again and again. *You are a home to yourself.* You are a home to Your Sexy. You get to throw away that which feels played out and unhealthy. You get to bring in that which feels yummy and uplifting. You get to decide when and how to open your home to visitors. And you get to decide who is allowed to stay for good. Promise to be gentle with yourself as you practice making choices on behalf of Your Sexy that are guided more by love and less by fear. You are a work in progress. We all are.

From your journey through the Map of Sexual Self-Awareness, you learned to cultivate from the inside-out:

- discernment regarding the ubiquitous messages about gender (*sex as cultural*)

- patience for the many chapters of your evolving sexual story (*sex as developmental*)

- commitment to practicing mindful and gentle awareness when you enter a sexual space (*sex as mental*)

- appreciation for your body, miraculous and imperfect (*sex as physical*)

- care for your feelings so you can hold pain and engage joy (*sex as emotional*)

- courage to turn toward your partner, seeing their complexity and sharing yours with them (*sex as relational*)

- awe for how profoundly connected you are to everything that has come before you, everything that will come after you, everything that lives within you, and everything that surrounds you (*sex as spiritual*).

In becoming a home to yourself, you create new possibilities for connection with your intimate partner(s). Your connection to Your

Sexy helps you navigate the hard stuff of intimate relationships: asking for what you need, clarifying what does not work for you, and listening to feedback. And your connection to Your Sexy opens you up to the good stuff of intimate relationships: pleasure, play, ecstasy, joy, teamwork, and comfort.

- Write a love letter to yourself about how you will take what you learned in this book and use it to guide you going forward.

- Talk with a sister, friend, or sexual partner about who Your Sexy aspires to be. Invite them to talk with you about who Their Sexy aspires to be. How might you provide each other with support and accountability?

As Marianne Williamson says, "Our deepest fear is that we are powerful beyond measure. It is our light, not our darkness that most frightens us. Your playing small does not serve the world. There is nothing enlightened about shrinking so that other people won't feel insecure around you."[181] Your Sexy shines brightest when she is trusted to be paradoxical—both shy and wild, both passive and unruly, both on-the-sidelines and center stage. Your Sexy dances with energy that is agentic and energy that is communal. Your Sexy is the girl, the witch, the scientist, the bitch, the artist, the dreamer, the heroine, the mother, the goddess. Your Sexy offers healing to her ancestors and forges a path for the girls who will follow her footsteps. Your Sexy dwells in possibility.

Acknowledgments

Writing a book is a journey. Writing a book about female sexuality is a journey full of both landmines and hidden treasures. I have been blessed every step of the way with fellow travelers, guides, cheerleaders, and guardian angels who righted me when I wobbled, held me when I cried, and pointed me in the right direction when I got lost.

Jennye Garibaldi, Jennifer Holder, Gretel Hakanson, Analis Souza, Jesse Burson, Cassie Kolias, Amy Shoup, Vicraj Gill, and Julie Bennett at New Harbinger have been fearless advocates for this book. My agent, Jill Marsal, has continued to support me in my writing endeavors. My publicist, Dana Kaye, brings clarity when I am confused and levity when I am discouraged.

Working at The Family Institute at Northwestern University means that I have access to people with bright minds and beautiful souls. Their input has helped me feel brave and clear. Steven Losardo, Rini Kaushal, Margaret Hensley, Toni Akunebu, and James Yoon sat with me in the early days of this project, helping me shape my thesis. This book would not have been possible without the best lab team ever assembled—JC Agundez, Lauren Attiah, Eliza Beth, Leah Fishbein, Kristen Herdegen, Rebecca Patterson, Kareigh Tieppo, Qinyi Zhu, and Angel Ziegler. Your words and love are on every page.

Hannah Miner, thank you for your artwork. Your talent adds great warmth to this book's tender journey.

Thank you to the colleagues who were generous with their wisdom and time. Rachel Zar, I'm in awe of your sharp mind and incisive editing. Michelle Herzog, I loved you as a student, and I love you as a colleague. Stephen Snyder, thank you your reflections and for your support. Adam Fisher, thank you for answering my texts patiently and promptly. Lori Brotto, when you agreed to write the foreword, I walked on air for days. I can't wait to return the favor to each and every one of you. Thank you also to my community of fellow love nerds (Esther Perel, Vienna Pharaon, Mark Groves, Dallas Hartwig, Jayson Gaddis,

Bela Gandhi, Eli Finkel, Sara Nasserzadeh, and Tasha Eurich) and my couples' group (Art Nielsen, Mona Fishbane, Rhonda Goldman, Jay Lebow, Steven Zuckerman, Charles Jaffe, David Klow, and Jennifer McComb). I love collaborating with you.

I was also blessed with early readers whose feedback was instrumental: Mollie Solomon, Matthew Solomon, Madeline Meyer, Hannah Miner, Giuliana Martinez, Patricia Herrera, Emily Forristel, Chao Qiao, Jasmine McCullough, and Noah Franklin.

I would be nothing without my female friendships—from elementary school, from my neighborhood, my gym friends, and my Circle Girls. The Sexy in me honors the Sexy in you.

Jamilli Alpuche, you are indispensable and so loved. Bonnie Lessing, you see me. Christine Reif, you taught a girl to love books and look what happened!

Our home is full—teenagers, a barky dog, schedules, careers, laughter, frustration, and so much love. So, when I invited this project into our orbit, everyone felt the effects. Courtney, your days of excitedly opening the packages that arrive on our doorstep ended promptly when you realized most shipments contained books about sex. For that, I am sorry. Brian, you could probably teach your health class with all of what you've learned from our dinnertime conversations. Thank you both for your patience and your check-ins. I hope someday this book serves you well. Todd, none of this is possible without you. You were sure about this book long before I was, and your steady belief gifted me courage. We are a quarter of a century into our love affair, and this book has deepened my appreciation of who we have been, who we are, and who I hope we will become.

Additional Resources
for Your Sexy

Books about Relationships

Eli Finkel, *The All-Or-Nothing Marriage: How the Best Marriages Work* (Penguin Random House, 2017).

John Gottman and Julie Schwartz Gottman, *Eight Dates: Essential Conversations for a Lifetime of Love* (Workman Publishing Company, 2019).

Sue Johnson, *Love Sense: The Revolutionary New Science of Romantic Relationships* (Little, Brown, and Company, 2013).

Esther Perel, *The State of Affairs: Rethinking Infidelity* (Harper, 2017).

Alexandra H. Solomon, *Loving Bravely: Twenty Lessons of Self-Discovery to Help You Get the Love You Want* (New Harbinger, 2017).

Stan Tatkin, *We Do: Saying Yes to a Relationships of Depth, True Connection, and Enduring Love* (Sounds True, 2018).

Books about Sexuality

Meg-John Barker, *Queer: A Graphic History* (Icon Books, 2016).

Kate Bornstein and S. Bear Bergman, *Gender Outlaws: The Next Generation* (Seal Press, 2010).

Lori Brotto, *Better Sex Through Mindfulness: How Women Can Cultivate Desire* (Greystone Books, 2018).

Betty Dodson, *Sex for One: The Joy of Selfloving* (Crown Trade Paperbacks, 1996).

Jaclyn Friedman and Jessica Valenti, *Yes Means Yes! Visions of Female Sexual Power and a World without Rape* (Seal Press, 2008).

Laci Green, *Sex Plus: Learning, Loving, and Enjoying Your Body* (HarperCollins, 2018).

Debby Herbenick, *Because It Feels Good: A Woman's Guide to Sexual Pleasure and Satisfaction* (Rodale Books, 2009).

Paul Joannides, *Guide to Getting It On: Unzipped* (Goofy Foot Press, 2017).

Ian Kerner, *Passionista: The Empowered Woman's Guide to Pleasuring a Man* (William Morrow Paperbacks, 2008).

Ian Kerner, *She Comes First: The Thinking Man's Guide to Pleasuring a Woman* (William Morrow Paperbacks, 2004).

Lindsay King-Miller, *Ask a Queer Chick: A Guide to Sex, Love, and Life for Girls Who Dig Girls* (Plume, 2016).

Marty Klein, *His Porn, Her Pain: Confronting America's PornPanic with Honest Talk about Sex* (Praeger, 2016).

David Ley, *Ethical Porn for Dicks: A Man's Ethical Guide for Viewing Pleasure* (ThreeL Media, 2016).

Audre Lorde, *Sister Outsider: Essays and Speeches* (Crossing Press, 1984).

Wednesday Martin, *Untrue: Why Nearly Everything We Everything We Believe about Women, Lust, and Infidelity Is Wrong and How the New Science Can Set Us Free* (Little, Brown, Spark, 2018).

Barry W. McCarthy and Emily J. McCarthy, *Rekindling Desire: A Step-by-Step Program to Help Low-Sex and No-Sex Marriages* (Brunner-Routledge, 2003).

Emily Nagoski, *Come as You Are: The Surprising New Science That Will Transform Your Sex Life* (Simon Schuster, 2015).

Gina Ogden and Jane Claypool, *The ABCs of Love and Sex: Expand Your Alphabet of Intimacy* (4-D Press, 2016).

Esther Perel, *Mating in Captivity: Unlocking Erotic Intelligence* (Harper, 2007).

Stephen Snyder, *Love Worth Making: How to Have Ridiculously Great Sex in a Long-Lasting Relationship* (St. Martin's Press, 2018).

Lauren Streicher, *Sex Rx: Hormones, Health and Your Best Sex Ever* (HarperCollins, 2015).

Regena Thomashauer, *Pussy: A Reclamation* (Hay House, Inc., 2016).

Bessel van der Kolk, *The Body Keeps the Score: Brain, Mind, and Body in the Healing of Trauma* (Viking, 2014).

Hida Viloria, *Born Both: An Intersex Life* (Hachette Books, 2017).

Books about Consensual Nonmonogamy

Janet Hardy and Dossie Easton, *The Ethical Slut: A Practical Guide to Polyamory, Open Relationships, and Other Freedoms in Sex and Love* (Penguin Random House, 2017).

Kathy Labriola, *The Jealousy Workbook: Exercises and Insights for Managing Open Relationships* (Greenery Press, 2013).

Tristan Taormino, *Opening Up: A Guide to Creating and Sustaining Open Relationships* (Cleis Press, 2008).

Franklin Veaux and Eve Rickert, *More Than Two: A Practical Guide to Ethical Polyamory* (Thorntree Press, 2014).

Books about Sex and Spirituality

Sera Beak, *Red Hot and Holy: A Heretic's Love Story* (Sounds True, 2013).

Barbara Carrellas, *Urban Tantra, Second Edition: Sacred Sex for the Twenty-First Century* (Penguin Random House, 2017).

Amy Jo Goddard, *Woman on Fire: Nine Elements to Wake Up Your Erotic Energy, Personal Power, and Sexual Intelligence* (Penguin Random House, 2015).

Linda Kay Klein. *Pure: Inside the Evangelical Movement that Shamed a Generation of Young Women and How I Broke Free* (Atria Books, 2018).

Thomas Moore, *The Soul of Sex: Cultivating Life as an Act of Love* (Harper Perennial, 1998).

Kristen J. Sollee, *Witches, Sluts, Feminists: Conjuring the Sex Positive* (ThreeL Media, 2017).

Websites

OMGYes (about the science of female pleasure)

O.school (a shame-free live-streaming platform for pleasure education)

Scarleteen (inclusive, comprehensive, supportive sexuality and relationships info for teens and emerging adults)

Feminist Erotica

Bright Desire

Dipsea

Feminist Porn Awards

I Feel Myself

Literotica

Make Love Not Porn

O'actually

Sssh

XConfessions (Erika Lust)

See also: Wear Your Voice's article "An Inclusive Porn Guide for the Marginalized" and Glamour's article "15 Porn Sites for Women That You'll Really, Really Enjoy"

Sexual Health Care

American Sexual Health Association (ASHA)

Centers for Disease Control (CDC)

Planned Parenthood (The website includes a chat feature, Roo, that provides answers to questions about sexual health.)

Rape, Abuse, and Incest National Network (RAINN)

Finding a Therapist

American Association of Sexuality Educators, Counselors, and Therapists (AASECT)

The Gottman Institute

International Centre for Excellence in Emotionally Focused Therapy (ICEEFT)

Psychology Today

Society for Sex Therapy and Research (SSTAR)

Endnotes

Chapter 1: From Outside-In to Inside-Out

1   Peggy Ornstein, *Girls and Sex: Navigating the Complicated Landscape* (New York: Harper, 2017).

2   Sophie Wilkinson, "Meet the Heroic Campaigners Making Cities Safer for Women," Refinery29 (May 19, 2016), http://www.refinery29.uk/women-safer-cities.

3   UN Women, "Facts and Figures: Ending Violence Against Women," (August 15, 2018), http://www.unwomen.org/en/what-we-do/ending-violence-against-women/facts-and-figures; The National Intimate Partner and Sexual Violence Survey, "NISVS: An Overview of 2010 Findings on Victimization by Sexual Orientation," https://www.cdc.gov/violenceprevention/pdf/cdc_nisvs_victimization_final-a.pdf.

4   #MeToo was originally created by activist Tarana Burke in 2007 to reach survivors of sexual violence in underprivileged communities. In the fall of 2017, actress Alyssa Milano reignited the hashtag on Twitter, and within forty-eight hours, there were nearly 1 million tweets. On Facebook, there were more than 12 million posts, comments, and reactions in less than twenty-four hours by 4.7 million users around the world who were sharing, many for the first time, that they too were survivors of unwanted sexual harassment, sexual abuse, and/or sexual assault.

5   As I have been working on this book, we have been witnessing a rollback of reproductive health care and access to abortions in the United States. I have experienced moments of panic, thinking, *How can I write a book about sexual pleasure in the midst of this war against women's rights?* Then I remember that now is precisely the time for us to declare without apology that bodily autonomy and self-determination are human rights. Retreating into fear and silence won't keep any of us safe.

Chapter 2: Relational Self-Awareness 101

6   I recognize that, for some people, "intersectional" is a hot-button term. For our purposes here, I am just wanting to highlight that we exist at the intersections of multiple identities.

7   Esther Perel, "The Secret to Desire in a Long-Term Relationship," TED video, 19:03, February 2013, https://www.ted.com/talks/esther_perel_the_secret_to_desire_in_a_long_term_relationship/transcript?language=en.

8   William M. Pinsof et al., *Integrative Systemic Therapy: Metaframeworks for Problem Solving with Individuals, Couples, and Family* (Washington, DC: American Psychological Association, 2017).

9   Masturbation tends to be solo sex (although sometimes done in a partner's presence). High-tech sex is arguably not sex between people. But you get my point!

10   Neale Donald Walsch, *Communion with God* (New York: TarcherPerigee, 2002), 71.

11   John M. Gottman and Nan Silver, *The Seven Principles for Making Marriage Work: A Practical Guide from the Country's Foremost Relationship Expert* (New York: Harmony Books, 2015).

Chapter 3: Of Warts, Bananas, and Birth Videos

12   Linda Kay Klein says that the object lesson with the tape is common when male and female students are in the classroom together. Her research indicates that when an object lesson is given *only* to girls, the focus is on being "used up" or "dirty." The metaphors include comparisons between a brand-new car and a broken-down car, an unused tissue and a snot-filled tissue, or a clear glass of water and a glass of water with food coloring added to it. The message to the girls is unmistakable: nobody will want you unless you are sexually pure. Linda K. Klein, *Pure: Inside the Evangelical Movement That Shamed a Generation of Young Women and How I Broke Free* (New York: Touchstone, 2018), 79.

13   The vast majority of LGBTQ+ youth never receive "The Talk" that they so desperately need and deserve, one that describes the sex that they will experience in their lives.

14   Richard Weissbourd et al., "The Talk: How Adults Can Promote Young People's Healthy Relationships and Prevent Misogyny and Sexual Harassment," *Harvard Graduate School of Education* 16 (2017): 8.

15   Christopher Trenholm et al., *Impacts of Four Title V, Section 510 Abstinence Education Programs* (Princeton, NJ: Mathematica Policy Research, 2007).

16   Peter S. Bearman and Hannah Brückner, "Promising the Future: Virginity Pledges and First Intercourse," *American Journal of Sociology* 106 (2001): 859–912; Arizona Department of Health Services, *Abstinence-Only Education Program: Fifth Year Evaluation Report* (Phoenix, AZ: Arizona Department of Health Services, 2003); Scott H. Frank, *Report on Abstinence-Only-Until-Marriage Programs in Ohio* (Cleveland, OH: Case Western Reserve University, School of Medicine, 2005); Hannah Brückner and Peter S. Bearman, "After the Promise: The STD Consequences of Adolescent Virginity Pledges," *Journal of Adolescent Health* 36, no. 4 (2005): 271–278.

17   Twitter, January 10, 2019, @DrSprankle.

18   Laura Santhanam, "Why the Federal Teen Pregnancy Prevention Program's Fate is Uncertain," PBS News Hour, March 22, 2018, https://www.pbs.org/newshour/health/why-the-federal-teen-pregnancy-prevention-programs-fate-is-uncertain.

19   Valerie Straus, "Trump Administration Cuts Funding for Pregnancy
      Prevention Programs. Here Are the Serious Consequences," *Washington Post*,
      September 7, 2017, https://www.washingtonpost.com/news/answer-sheet/
      wp/2017/09/07/
      trump-administration-cuts-funding-for-teen-pregnancy-prevention-programs-
      here-are-the-serious-consequences/?utm_term=.74c8ecfc5a4b.

20   Centers for Disease Control and Prevention, *School Health Profiles 2014*, 2015,
      https://www.cdc.gov/healthyyouth/data/profiles/pdf/2014/2014_profiles_
      report.pdf.

21   Guttmacher Institute, "Fewer US Teens Are Getting Formal Sex Education
      Than in the Past," April 14, 2016, https://www.guttmacher.org/news-
      release/2016/fewer-us-teens-are-receiving-formal-sex-education-now-past.

22   Chantell Ivanski and Taylor Kohut, "Exploring Definitions of Sex Positivity
      through Thematic Analysis," *The Canadian Journal of Human Sexuality* 26,
      no. 3 (December 2017): 216–225. (Quote is from p. 216.)

23   Sex education that is inclusive of LGBTQ+ students helps everyone.
      Currently, only 6.7 percent of LGBTQ+ students received sex education that
      included positive representations of LGBTQ+ topics. *The 2017 National
      School Climate Survey: The Experiences of Lesbian, Gay, Bisexual, Transgender,
      and Queer Youth in Our Nation's Schools*, https://www.glsen.org/sites/default/
      files/GLSEN%202017%20National%20School%20Climate%20Survey%20
      %28NSCS%29%20-%20Executive%20Summary%20%28English%29.pdf.
      This is true even though 85 percent of parents of high schoolers (and 78
      percent of parents of middle schoolers) support including discussions of
      sexual orientation in sex ed. "Let's Talk Poll," New York: Planned Parenthood
      Federation of America and Center for Latino Adolescent and Family Health,
      2015. In such cases, students who identify as LGBTQ+ feel seen, valued, and
      prepared to make healthy choices, and students who identify as straight are
      given an opportunity to normalize differences, inviting them to be more
      compassionate with the myriad ways that we all exist outside of the dominant
      paradigms.

24   CNM is defined as an agreement that one or both members of a couple may
      pursue sexual or romantic experiences outside of the relationship.

Chapter 4: Living and Loving in a Patriarchy

25   Kimberlé Crenshaw, "Demarginalizing the Intersection of Race and Sex: A
      Black Feminist Critique of Antidiscrimination Doctrine, Feminist Theory,
      and Antiracist Politics," *University of Chicago Legal Forum* 1, no. 8 (1989):
      139–167, https://chicagounbound.uchicago.edu/uclf/vol1989/iss1/8/.

26   Audre Lorde, "Learning from the 60s," in *Sister Outsider: Essays and Speeches
      by Audre Lorde* (Berkeley, CA: Crossing Press, 2007), 138.

27   Sara McClelland, "Intimate Justice," in *Encyclopedia of Critical Psychology*, ed.
      Thomas Teo (London: Springer Reference, 2014), 1010–1013. (Quote from
      page 1010.)

28   Also take a look at the Gender Unicorn created by the group Trans Student Educational Resources, which expands these concepts a bit more.

29   Some people prefer to say "sex assigned at birth" rather than "biological sex."

30   Claire C. Miller, "How Same-Sex Couples Divide Chores, and What It Reveals about Modern Parenting," *New York Times*, May 16, 2018, https://www.nytimes.com/2018/05/16/upshot/same-sex-couples-divide-chores-much-more-evenly-until-they-become-parents.html.

31   Kenneth Matos, "Modern Families: Same- and Different-Sex Couples Negotiating at Home," 2015, http://www.familiesandwork.org/downloads/modern-families.pdf.

32   Andrea E. Abele and Bogdan Wojciszke, "Communal and Agentic Content in Social Cognition: A Dual Perspective Model," *Advances in Experimental Social Psychology* 50 (2014): 195–255.

33   Dan P. McAdams, "Coding Autobiographical Episodes for Themes of Agency and Communion," unpublished manuscript, Northwestern University, Evanston, IL (2001).

34   Emily S. Lefkowitz and Peter B. Zeldow, "Masculinity and Femininity Predict Optimal Mental Health: A Belated Test of the Androgyny Hypothesis," *Journal of Personality Assessment* 87 (2006): 95–101.

35   Leslie S. Greenberg and Rhonda N. Goldman, *Emotion-Focused Couples Therapy: The Dynamics of Emotion, Love, and Power* (Washington, DC: American Psychological Association, 2008).

36   Joel Y. Wong et al., "Meta-Analyses of the Relationship between Conformity to Masculine Norms and Mental Health-Related Outcomes," *Journal of Counseling Psychology* 64 (2017): 80–93.

37   Terry Real, "The Resurgence of Patriarchy," *Psychotherapy Networker*, 2017, https://www.psychotherapynetworker.org/blog/details/1302/the-resurgence-of-patriarchy.

38   Michael J. Marks and Kassia Wosick, "Exploring College Men's and Women's Attitudes about Women's Sexuality and Pleasure via Their Perceptions of Female Novelty Party Attendees," *Sex roles* 77 (2017): 550–561; Deana A. Rohlinger, "Eroticizing Men: Cultural Influences on Advertising and Male Objectification," *Sex Roles* 46 (2002): 61–74.

39   However, you do not need to forsake erotica altogether, as there is plenty of inclusive, ethical, and feminist content. The "Additional Resources for Your Sexy" section in this book will point you toward some fabulously empowered "dirtiness."

40   RAINN (Rape Abuse, and Incest National Network), "What Consent Looks Like," https://www.rainn.org/articles/what-is-consent.

Chapter 5: Your Sexy Is a Glorious and Unfolding Story

41   Kristen P. Mark and Julie A. Lasslo, "Maintaining Sexual Desire in Long-Term Relationships: A Systematic Review and Conceptual Model," *The Journal of Sex Research* 55 (2018): 563–581.

42   Helen S. Kaplan, *Disorders of Sexual Desire* (New York: Simon and Schuster, 1979).

43   Edward O. Laumann, Anthony Paik, and Raymond C. Rosen, "Sexual Dysfunction in the United States: Prevalence and Predictors," *JAMA* 281 (1999): 537–544.

44   Rosemary Basson, "Rethinking Low Sexual Desire in Women," *BJOG: An International Journal of Obstetrics & Gynecology* 109 (2002): 357–363.

45   Basson, "Rethinking Low Sexual Desire in Women," 357.

46   Basson, "Rethinking Low Sexual Desire in Women," 357.

47   Sarah H. Murray et al., "A Qualitative Exploration of Factors that Affect Sexual Desire among Men Aged 30 to 65 in Long-Term Relationships," *The Journal of Sex Research* 54 (2017): 319–330.

48   Krzysztof Nowosielski, Beata Wróbel, and Robert Kowalczyk, "Women's Endorsement of Models of Sexual Response: Correlates and Predictors," *Archives of Sexual Behavior* 45 (2016): 291–302. Note that their research participants, like most research participants in studies like these, were heterosexually partnered women, so I just want to say to readers who identify as lesbian and who live beyond the binary, I see you! Change is coming, but it's slow.

49   Emily Nagoski, *Come as You Are: The Surprising New Science that Will Transform Your Sex Life* (New York: Simon and Schuster, 2015).

50   John Bancroft, "Sexual Science in the 21st Century: Where Are We Going?" *Journal of Sex Research* 36 (1999): 226–229; John Bancroft and Erick Janssen, "The Dual Control Model of Male Sexual Response: A Theoretical Approach to Centrally Mediated Erectile Dysfunction," *Neuroscience Biobehavioral Reviews* 24 (2000): 571–579.

51   Blair Hodgson et al., "Using the Dual Control Model to Investigate the Relationship between Mood, Genital, and Self-Reported Sexual Arousal in Men and Women," *The Journal of Sex Research* 53 (2016): 979–993.

52   Byron Katie with Stephen Mitchell, *Loving What Is: Four Questions that Can Change Your Life* (New York: Harmony Books, 2002), 2.

53   Sarah Murray and Robin Milhausen, "Factors Impacting Women's Sexual Desire: Examining Long-Term Relationships in Emerging Adulthood," *The Canadian Journal of Human Sexuality* 21 (2012): 101–116.

54   Amy Muise et al., "Understanding When a Partner Is Not in the Mood: Sexual Communal Strength in Couples Transitioning to Parenthood," *Archives of Sexual Behavior* 46 (2017): 1993–2006.

55   Muise et al., "Understanding When a Partner Is Not in the Mood."

56   Julia O'Loughlin, Rosemary Basson, and Lori A. Brotto, "Women with Hypoactive Sexual Desire Disorder Versus Sexual Interest/Arousal Disorder: An Empirical Test of Raising the Bar," *The Journal of Sex Research* 55 (2018): 734–746.

57   Elizabeth A. Armstrong, Paula England, and Alison C. K. Fogarty, "Orgasm in College Hookups and Relationships," in *Families as They Really Are*, ed. Barbara J. Risman (New York, NY: Norton, 2010), 362–377.

58   Nick Anderson and Scott Clement, "1 in 5 College Women Say They Were Violated," *The Washington Post*, June 12, 2015, http://www.washingtonpost.com/sf/local/2015/06/12/1-in-5-women-say-they-were-violated/.

59   Elizabeth A. Armstrong, Paula England, and Alison C. K. Fogarty, "Accounting for Women's Orgasm and Sexual Enjoyment in College Hookups and Relationships," *American Sociological Review* 77 (2012): 435–462.

60   Armstrong, England, and Fogarty, "Accounting for Women's Orgasm and Sexual Enjoyment."

61   Mark Regnerus, *Forbidden Fruit: Sex and Religion in the Lives of American Teenagers* (Oxford: Oxford University Press, 2007).

62   Armstrong, England, and Fogarty, "Accounting for Women's Orgasm and Sexual Enjoyment," 438.

Chapter 6: What You Think Matters

63   Esther Perel, *Mating in Captivity: Unlocking Erotic Intelligence* (New York: Harper, 2007).

64   Westerners need to be humble enough to acknowledge that in parts of the world, specifically countries in Asia, mindfulness has been practiced for thousands of years. Westerners may be the first to use brain scans to show that mindfulness "works," but the monks of Tibet have known for thousands of years that it does!

65   Daphne M. Davis and Jeffrey A. Hayes, "What Are the Benefits of Mindfulness," *Monitor on Psychology* 43 (2012): 64, https://www.apa.org/monitor/2012/07-08/ce-corner.

66   Lori A. Brotto and Rosemary Basson, "Group Mindfulness-Based Therapy Significantly Improves Sexual Desire in Women," *Behaviour Research and Therapy* 57 (2014): 43–54.

67   Eva Elmerstig, Barbro Wijma, and Katarina Swahnberg, "Prioritizing the Partner's Enjoyment: A Population-Based Study on Young Swedish Women with Experience of Pain During Vaginal Intercourse," *Journal of Psychosomatic Obstetrics & Gynecology* 34 (2013): 82–89.

68   Michelle N. Lafrance, Monika Stelzl, and Kristen Bullock, "'I'm Not Gonna Fake It': University Women's Accounts of Resisting the Normative Practice of Faking Orgasm," *Psychology of Women Quarterly* 41 (2017): 210–222.

69   Kristin Neff, *Self-Compassion: The Proven Power of Being Kind to Yourself* (New York: HarperCollins, 2011).

70   Kristin Neff, *Self-Compassion.*

71   Harpo Studios (producer). *The Oprah Winfrey Show*, television broadcast. Chicago, IL: King World Productions, November 2, 1994.

72   Donna Freitas, *The End of Sex: How Hookup Culture Is Leaving a Generation Unhappy, Sexually Unfulfilled, and Confused About Intimacy* (New York: Basic Books, 2013).

Chapter 7: It's Time to Be Sweet to *All* of You

73   The process is called vaginal bleaching, but this is an incorrect name. The vagina is the muscular tube that leads from the external genitals to the cervix. What is being bleached in this process is the outer labia or labia majora.

74   Renee Engeln, *Beauty Sick: How the Cultural Obsession with Appearance Hurts Girls and Women* (New York: Harper, 2017).

75   Audre Lorde, *A Burst of Light: And Other Essays* (Ann Arbor, MI: Firebrand Books, 1988), 130.

76   Engeln, *Beauty Sick*, 30.

77   Engeln, *Beauty Sick*, 30.

78   "Eating Disorders in LGBTQ+ Populations," National Eating Disorders Association, https://www.nationaleatingdisorders.org/learn/general-information/lgbtq.

79   Brené Brown, *Rising Strong: The Reckoning. The Rumble. The Revolution* (New York, NY: Spiegel & Grau, 2015), 195.

80   Carrie Kerpen, "Stop Comparing Your Behind-the-Scenes with Everyone's Highlight Reel," *Forbes*, July 19, 2017, https://www.forbes.com/sites/carriekerpen/2017/07/29/stop-comparing-your-behind-the-scenes-with-everyones-highlight-reel/#51ed12613a07.

81   Adriana M. Manago et al., "Facebook Involvement, Objectified Body Consciousness, Body Shame, and Sexual Assertiveness in College Women and Men," *Sex Roles* 72 (2015), 1–14; Davide Marengo et al., "Highly-Visual Social Media and Internalizing Symptoms in Adolescence: The Mediating Role of Body Image Concerns," *Computers in Human Behavior* 82 (2018): 63–69.

82   J. K. Rowling, *Harry Potter and the Sorcerer's Stone* (New York: Scholastic, Inc., 1997), 216.

83   Jill Huppert et al., "College Men Lack Basic Knowledge About Gynecology," *Journal of Pediatric and Adolescent Gynecology* 24 (2011): e47.

84   Vanessa R. Schick et al., "Genital Appearance Dissatisfaction: Implications for Women's Genital Image Self-Consciousness, Sexual Esteem, Sexual Satisfaction, and Sexual Risk," *Psychology of Women Quarterly* 34 (2010): 394–404.

85   Nagoski, *Come as You Are*, 5.

86   Jamie McCartney, "The Great Wall of Vagina," https://jamiemccartney.com/portfolio/the-great-wall-of-vagina/.

87   Just a quick reminder that the cervix is the passageway from the vagina to the uterus. IUDs hang out just above the cervix, and the cervix is what gets swabbed during a gynecological exam.

88   Karen Horton, "Stats Show Labiaplasty Is Becoming More Popular," *American Society of Plastic Surgeons*, April 25, 2017, https://www.plasticsurgery.org/news/blog/stats-show-labiaplasty-is-becoming-more-popular.

89   Lisa J. Moore and Adele E. Clarke, "Clitoral Conventions and Transgressions: Graphic Representations in Anatomy Texts, C1900–1991," *Feminist Studies* 21 (1995): 255–301.

90   For a thorough history of the clitoris's vanishing act and how we can make up for lost time, check out the fabulous Cliteracy project (http://www.sophiawallace.com) by artist Sophia Wallace.

91   Helen E. O'Connell et al., "Anatomical Relationship between Urethra and Clitoris," *The Journal of Urology* 159 (1998): 1892–1897.

92   Nagoski, *Come as You Are*, 21.

93   Debby Herbenick et al., "Women's Experiences with Genital Touching, Sexual Pleasure, and Orgasm: Results from a U.S. Probability Sample of Women Ages 18 to 94," *Journal of Sex & Marital Therapy* 44 (2018): 201–212.

94   Asexuality is defined as a lack of sexual attraction to other people or a low or absent interest in or desire for sexual activity. Some have argued that asexuality is an unchosen and biologically based identity like any other, and others have wondered if asexuality is, for some, a kind of rebellion against mandated heterosexuality.

95   Stephen Snyder, *Love Worth Making: How to Have Ridiculously Great Sex in a Lasting Relationship* (New York: St. Martin's Press, 2018).

96   Sigmund Freud, *New Introductory Lectures on Psycho-Analysis* (London: The Hogarth Press and the Institute for Psychoanalysis, 1933).

97   Debby Herbenick, *Because It Feels Good: A Woman's Guide to Sexual Pleasure and Satisfaction* (New York: Rodale Books, 2009).

98   Herbenick, *Because It Feels Good*, 107.

99   Justin R. Garcia et al., "Variation in Orgasm Occurrence by Sexual
      Orientation in a Sample of U.S. Singles," *The Journal of Sexual Medicine* 11
      (2014): 2645–2652.

100   Christine E. Kaestle and Katherine R. Allen, "The Role of Masturbation in
      Healthy Sexual Development: Perceptions of Young Adults," *Archives of
      Sexual Behavior* 40 (2011): 983–994.

101   Breanne Fahs and Eric Swank, "Adventures with the 'Plastic Man': Sex Toys,
      Compulsory Heterosexuality, and the Politics of Women's Sexual Pleasure,"
      Sexuality & Culture 17 (2013): 666–685.

Chapter 8: Your Feelings Are Data

102   Greenberg and Goldman, *Emotion-Focused Couples Therapy* (Washington,
      DC: America Psychological Association, 2008)

103   Robert D. Schweitzer, Jessica O'Brien, and Andrea Burri, "Postcoital
      Dysphoria: Prevalence and Psychological Correlates," *Sexual Medicine* 3
      (2015): 235–243.

104   Joel Maczkowiack and Robert D. Schweitzer, "Postcoital Dysphoria:
      Prevalence and Correlates among Males," *Journal of Sex & Marital Therapy* 3
      (2019): 1–13.

105   Richard A. Friedman, "Sex and Depression: In the Brain, If Not the Mind,"
      New York Times. January 19, 2009, https://www.nytimes.com/2009/01/20/
      health/views/20mind.html.

106   Brené Brown, *The Gifts of Imperfection: Let Go of Who You Think You're
      Supposed to Be and Embrace Who You Are* (Center City, MN: Hazelden
      Publishing, 2010), 70.

107   Twenty-one percent of heterosexual men, 40 percent of gay men, and 47
      percent of bisexual men have experienced sexual trauma (HRC.org).

108   Jackson Katz, "Violence Against Women—It's a Men's Issue" TED video,
      17:37, November 2012, https://www.ted.com/talks/ackson_katz_violence_
      against_women_it_s_a_men_s_issue/up-next.

109   Judith Leavitt, *The Sexual Alarm System: Women's Unwanted Response to
      Sexual Intimacy and How to Overcome It* (Lanham, MD: Jason Aronson,
      2012).

110   Bessel A. van der Kolk, *The Body Keeps the Score: Brain, Mind, and Body in
      the Healing of Trauma* (New York: Viking, 2014).

111   Donna Eden and David Feinstein, *Energy Medicine: Balancing Your Body's
      Energies for Optimal Health, Joy, and Vitality* (New York: TarcherPerigree,
      2008).

Chapter 9: The Space Between You and Your Partner

112   Even if you practice CNM, you still may have a primary relationship in which you return again and again have to sex with the same partner.

113   Susan Sprecher et al., "Sexual Satisfaction and Sexual Expression as Predictors of Relationship Satisfaction and Stability," in *The Handbook of Sexuality in Close Relationships*, ed. John H. Harvey, Amy Wenzel, and Susan Sprecher (Mahwah, NJ: Lawrence Erlbaum Associates, Inc, 2004), 235–256; Susan S. Hendrick and Clyde Hendrick, "Sex and Romantic Love: Connects and Disconnects," in *The Handbook of Sexuality in Close Relationships*, ed. John H. Harvey, Amy Wenzel, and Susan Sprecher (Mahwah, NJ: Lawrence Erlbaum Associates, Inc, 2004), 159–182; Diane Holmberg, Karen L. Blair, and Maggie Phillips, "Women's Sexual Satisfaction as a Predictor of Well-Being in Same-Sex Versus Mixed-Sex Relationships," *Journal of Sex Research* 47 (2010): 1–11.

114   Barry W. McCarthy and L. Elizabeth Bodnar, "The Equity Model of Sexuality: Navigating and Negotiating the Similarities and Differences between Men and Women in Sexual Behaviour, Roles and Values," *Sexual and Relationship Therapy* 20 (2005): 225–235.

115   James K. McNulty, Carolyn A. Wenner, and Terri D. Fisher, "Longitudinal Associations among Relationship Satisfaction, Sexual Satisfaction, and Frequency of Sex in Early Marriage," *Archives of Sexual Behavior* 45 (2016): 85–97; Dietrich Klusmann, "Sexual Motivation and the Duration of Partnership," *Archives of Sexual Behavior* 31 (2002): 275–287.

116   Daniel Siegel, *Mindsight: The New Science of Personal Transformation* (New York: Bantam, 2010).

117   Anthony F. Bogaert and Lori A. Brotto, "Object of Desire Self-Consciousness Theory," *Journal of Sex and Marital Therapy* 40 (2014): 323–338.

118   Anthony F. Bogaert, Beth A. Visser, and Julie A. Pozzebon, "Gender Differences in Object of Desire Self-Consciousness Sexual Fantasies," *Archives of Sexual Behavior* 44 (2015): 2299–2310.

119   Daniel Bergner, "What Do Women Want?" *New York Times*, January 22, 2001, https://www.nytimes.com/2009/01/25/magazine/25desire-t.html.

120   Justin J. Lehmiller, *Tell Me What You Want: The Science of Sexual Desire and How It Can Help You Improve Your Sex Life* (New York: Da Capo Press, 2018).

121   Lehmiller, *Tell Me What You Want*.

122   Lehmiller, *Tell Me What You Want*, p. xiii.

123   Jack Morin, *The Erotic Mind: Unlocking the Inner Sources of Passion and Fulfillment* (New York: Harper Perennial, 1996).

124   Lehmiller, *Tell Me What You Want*.

125 David A. Frederick et al., "What Keeps Passion Alive? Sexual Satisfaction Is Associated with Sexual Communication, Mood Setting, Sexual Variety, Oral Sex, Orgasm, and Sex Frequency in a National U.S. Study," *The Journal of Sex Research* 54 (2017): 186–201.

126 Andrea S. Miller and Sandra E. Byers, "Actual and Desired Duration of Foreplay and Intercourse: Discordance and Misperceptions within Heterosexual Couples," *Journal of Sex Research* 41, no. 3 (2004): 301–309.

127 Allen B. Mallory, Amelia M. Stanton, and Ariel B. Handy, "Couples' Sexual Communication and Dimensions of Sexual Function: A Meta-Analysis," *The Journal of Sex Research*, https://doi.org/10.1080/00224499.2019.1568375.

128 Susan Johnson, "The Three Kinds of Sex," http://www.drsuejohnson.com/the-three-kinds-of-sex/.

129 Tammy Nelson, Psychotherapy Networker Symposium, March 17, 2016.

130 Perel, *Mating in Captivity.*

131 Charlene L. Muehlenhard and Sheena K. Shippee, "Men's and Women's Reports of Pretending Orgasm," *The Journal of Sex Research* 47, no. 6 (2010): 552–567.

132 Muehlenhard and Shippee, "Men's and Women's Reports of Pretending Orgasm."

133 The predominant sexual script portrays men as always ready, willing, and able, obliterating the reality that relational safety and trust help men relax into a sexual experience. A friend of mine struggled with erection and orgasm during his one-night stands, and he experienced a massive offloading of shame when he simply accepted, "It turns out that there's a direct line from my penis to my heart."

134 Kaethe Weingarten, "The Discourses of Intimacy: Adding a Social Constructionist and Feminist View," *Family Process* 30, no. 3 (1991): 285–305.

135 Perel, *Mating in Captivity,* 219.

Chapter 10: Sex as Transcendence

136 Froma Walsh, *Spiritual Resources in Family Therapy* 2nd ed. (New York: The Guilford Press, 2009), 5.

137 Walsh, *Spiritual Resources in Family Therapy,* 5.

138 Pierre Teilhard de Chardin, *Toward the Future* (Wilmington, MA: Mariner Books, 1975), 79.

139 Harold G. Koenig, Dana E. King, and Verna B. Carson, *Handbook of Religion and Health* (New York: Oxford University Press, 2012).

140 Pew Research Center, "When Americans Say They Believe in God, What Do They Mean?" April 25, 2018, http://www.pewforum.org/2018/04/25/when-americans-say-they-believe-in-god-what-do-they-mean/.

141 Pew Research Center, "When Americans Say They Believe in God."

142 Pew Research Center, "Young Adults Around the World Are Less Religious by Several Measures," June 13, 2018, http://www.pewforum.org/2018/06/13/young-adults-around-the-world-are-less-religious-by-several-measures/.

143 Lehmiller, *Tell Me What You Want*, 107.

144 Donna Freitas, *Sex and the Soul: Juggling Sexuality, Spirituality, Romance, and Religion on America's College Campuses* (New York: Oxford Press, 2008).

145 Klein, *Pure*.

146 Jessica Valenti, *The Purity Myth: How America's Obsession with Virginity Is Hurting Young Women* (New York: Seal Press, 2009).

147 Barbara Carrellas, *Urban Tantra, Second Edition: Sacred Sex for the Twenty-First Century* (New York: Ten Speed Press, 2017), 8.

148 Carrellas, *Urban Tantra*, 11.

Chapter 11: Your Grandma Never Swiped Right

149 Stephanie Coontz, *Marriage, a History: How Love Conquered Marriage* (New York: Penguin Books, 2006).

150 Jane E. Myers, Jayamala Madathil, and Lynne R. Tingle, "Marriage Satisfaction and Wellness in India and the United States: A Preliminary Comparison of Arranged Marriages and Marriages of Choice," *Journal of Counseling & Development* 83 (2005): 183–190.

151 If you are the product of your parents' arranged marriage, but you've been raised in a Western world that elevates love above all else, you may feel caught in not just a generation gap but a cultural one as well. That shift from role-to-role to soul-to-soul is deeply personal for you. Like many of my first-generation students and clients, you likely carry a desire to hold *both* your deep loyalty to family *and* your reality that your approach to love differs from theirs. You deserve a partner who empathizes with how tender this conflict may be for you even if it is unfamiliar to them.

152 The newfound possibilities in the lives of women exist alongside the reality that many women continue to struggle with ways in which feminist movements historically left behind, or purposely excluded, women of color and other marginalized women (for example, trans women and poor women). Therefore, discussion of these sociological shifts must be ever-contextualized within the reality of ongoing systems of oppression that impact both the public-facing and intimate lives of women.

153 Hanna Rosin, "Boys on the Side," *The Atlantic*, September 2012, https://www.theatlantic.com/magazine/archive/2012/09/boys-on-the-side/309062/.

154 Coontz, *Marriage, A History*.

155   Gretchen Livingston and Anna Brown, "Intermarriage in the U.S. Fifty Years After Loving v. Virginia" Pew Research Center, May 18, 2017, http://www.pewsocialtrends.org/2017/05/18/1-trends-and-patterns-in-intermarriage/.

156   Richard G. Wight, Allen J. LeBlanc, and M. V. Lee Badgett, "Same-Sex Legal Marriage and Psychological Well-Being: Findings from the California Health Interview Survey," *American Journal of Public Health* 103 (2013): 339–346.

157   U.S. census data show that in 1960, 68 percent of all twenty-somethings were married, but in 2008, only 26 percent were. *The Decline of Marriage and Rise of New Families*, Pew Research Center, November 18, 2010, http://www.pewsocialtrends.org/2010/11/18/the-decline-of-marriage-and-rise-of-new-families/2/.

158   In a sample of over two thousand Millennials, 70 percent reported that they wanted to get married (25 percent were not sure, and 5 percent stated that they do not want to get married). In addition, 75 percent shared that they want to have children (19 percent were not sure, and 7 percent stated that they do not want to have children). Pew Research Center, *The Decline of Marriage and Rise of New Families*, November 18, 2010; Wendy Wang and Kim Parker, *"Record Share of Americans Have Never Married: As Values, Economics, and Gender Patterns Change,"* Pew Research Center, September 24, 2014, http://www.pewsocialtrends.org/2014/09/24/record-share-of-americans-have-never-married/.

159   Andrew Cherlin, *Marriage Go Round: The State of Marriage and Family in America Today* (New York: Vintage, 2010).

160   Jeffrey J. Arnett, *Emerging Adulthood: The Winding Road from the Late Teens through the Twenties* (Oxford: Oxford University Press, 2014).

161   Shawn Carter, "30 Something," audio track on *Kingdom Come*, Roc-A-Fella, Def Jam, 2006.

162   Ivan Boszormenyi-Nagy and Geraldine M. Spark, *Invisible Loyalties: Reciprocity in Intergenerational Family Therapy* (New York: Routlege, 1984).

163   Claire C. Miller, "The Divorce Surge Is Over, but the Myth Lives On," *New York Times*, December 2, 2014, https://www.nytimes.com/2014/12/02/upshot/the-divorce-surge-is-over-but-the-myth-lives-on.html.

164   Denise S. Bartell, "Influence of Parental Divorce on Romantic Relationships in Young Adulthood: A Cognitive-Developmental Perspective," in *Handbook of Divorce and Relationship Dissolution*, ed. Mark A. Fine and John H. Harvey (Mahwah, NJ: Erlbaum, 2006), 339–360.

165   Ming Cui, Frank D. Fincham, and Jared A. Durtschi, "The Effect of Parental Divorce on Young Adults' Romantic Relationship Dissolution: What Makes a Difference?" *Personal Relationships* 18 (2011): 410–426.

166   Janet Hardy and Dossie Easton, *The Ethical Slut: A Practical Guide to Polyamory, Open Relationships, and Other Freedoms in Sex and Love* (New York: Ten Speed Press, 2017).

167   Amy C. Moors, "Has the American Public's Interest in Information Related to Relationships Beyond 'the Couple' Increased over Time?" *The Journal of Sex Research* 54 (2017): 677–684.

168   Peter Moore, "Young Americans Are Less Wedded to Monogamy Than Their Elders," *YouGov*, October 3, 2016, https://today.yougov.com/topics/lifestyle/articles-reports/2016/10/03/young-americans-less-wedded-monogamy.

169   It is an unfortunate reality that individuals and couples make these choices in a climate that still judges women more harshly than men for seeking nontraditional sexual choices.

170   Alyssa Giacobbe, "Women Are Now Cheating as Much as Men, but with Fewer Consequences," *New York Magazine*, May 26, 2016, http://nymag.com/betamale/2016/05/women-are-now-cheating-as-much-as-men-but-with-fewer-consequences.html.

171   The breakneck pace of technological advances means that we will continue to be confronted with new twists on these questions.

172   Aaron Smith and Maeve Duggan, "Online Dating & Relationships," Pew Research Center, October 21, 2013, http://www.pewinternet.org/2013/10/21/online-dating-relationships/.

173   John T. Cacioppo et al., "Marital Satisfaction and Break-Ups Differ across On-Line and Off-Line Meeting Venues," *Proceedings of the National Academy of Sciences* 110 (2013): 10135–10140.

174   Barry Schwartz, *The Paradox of Choice: Why Less Is More* (New York: EccoPress, 2016).

175   John Travis Spoede Jr., Stephanie Ellis, and Ron Homann, "Effort, Depth, Satisfaction, and Resilience across the Spectrum of Online-to-Offline Relationships," *Journal of Management Science and Business Intelligence* 1 (2016): 27–36; Artemio Ramirez et al., "When Online Dating Partners Meet Offline: The Effect of Modality Switching on Relational Communication between Online Daters," *Journal of Computer-Mediated Communication* 20 (2014): 99–114.

Chapter 12: Reflections for Men Who Love Women Who Are Taking Sexy Back

176   Terry Real, "Why Men Struggle with Intimacy," https://goop.com/work/relationships/why-men-struggle-with-intimacy/.

177   *The Mask You Live In*, directed by Jennifer Siebel Newsom (The Representation Project, 2015). Documentary.

178   Remember that your sexuality is about so much more than to whom you are attracted and what you do or don't do with your genitals. Your sexuality is an essential part of who you are and is about how you do touch, connection, closeness, power, and pleasure.

179   Mona DeKoven Fishbane, *Loving with the Brain in Mind: Neurobiology &*
       Couple Therapy (New York, NY: W.W. Norton & Company, Inc, 2013).

180   Quote Investigator, "They May Forget What You Said, But They Will Never
       Forget How You Made Them Feel," https://quoteinvestigator.com/2014/04/06/
       they-feel/#note-8611-15.

Chapter 13: Welcome Home, Sexy

181   Marianne Williamson, *A Return to Love: Reflections on the Principles of a*
       Course in Miracles (San Francisco, CA: HarperOne, 1996), 190.

Alexandra H. Solomon, PhD, is on faculty in the Weinberg College of Arts and Sciences, and the School of Education and Social Policy at Northwestern University. She is a licensed clinical psychologist at The Family Institute at Northwestern University, and is on faculty at The Omega Institute. Her first book, *Loving Bravely*, was featured on *The Today Show*. She writes articles and chapters for leading academic journals and books in the field of marriage and family. She maintains a psychotherapy practice for individual adults and couples, teaches and trains marriage and family therapy graduate students, and teaches the internationally renowned undergraduate course, "Building Loving and Lasting Relationships: Marriage 101." Solomon is a highly sought-after speaker who works with groups like the United States Military Academy at West Point, Microsoft, and the American Association for Marriage and Family Therapy. She is frequently asked to talk about love, sex, and marriage for media outlets like *O, The Oprah Magazine*; *The Atlantic*; *Vogue*; NPR; and *Scientific American*. She is an international speaker and teacher whose work has been featured on five continents. She lives in the Greater Chicago Area.

Foreword writer **Lori Brotto, PhD,** is executive director of the Women's Health Research Institute in Vancouver, BC, Canada. Her research focuses on advancing the science of psychological and mindfulness-based interventions for women's sexual health. She is author of *Better Sex Through Mindfulness*.

Real change *is* possible

For more than forty-five years, New Harbinger has published proven-effective self-help books and pioneering workbooks to help readers of all ages and backgrounds improve mental health and well-being, and achieve lasting personal growth. In addition, our spirituality books offer profound guidance for deepening awareness and cultivating healing, self-discovery, and fulfillment.

Founded by psychologist Matthew McKay and Patrick Fanning, New Harbinger is proud to be an independent, employee-owned company. Our books reflect our core values of integrity, innovation, commitment, sustainability, compassion, and trust. Written by leaders in the field and recommended by therapists worldwide, New Harbinger books are practical, accessible, and provide real tools for real change.

newharbingerpublications

MORE BOOKS *from*
NEW HARBINGER PUBLICATIONS

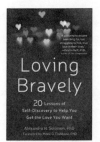

Register your **new harbinger** titles for additional benefits!

When you register your **new harbinger** title—purchased in any format, from any source—you get access to benefits like the following:

- Downloadable accessories like printable worksheets and extra content
- Instructional videos and audio files
- Information about updates, corrections, and new editions

Not every title has accessories, but we're adding new material all the time.

Access free accessories in 3 easy steps:

1. Sign in at NewHarbinger.com (or **register** to create an account).

2. Click on **register a book**. Search for your title and click the **register** button when it appears.

3. Click on the **book cover or title** to go to its details page. Click on **accessories** to view and access files.

That's all there is to it!

If you need help, visit:

NewHarbinger.com/accessories

new harbinger
CELEBRATING
40 YEARS